# Formula1 '99 technical analysis

by Giorgio Piola

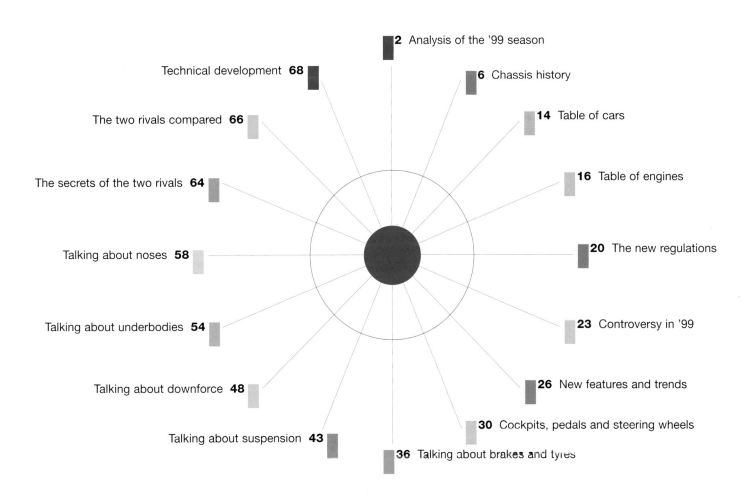

GIORGIO NADA EDITORE

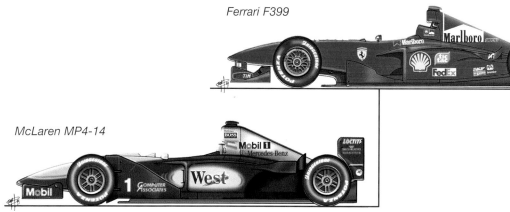

*Ferrari F399*

*McLaren MP4-14*

From a strictly technical point of view the 1999 season was rather less interesting than the '98 edition enlivened by the introduction of two important modifications to the technical regulations: the narrowing of the maximum permitted width, and therefore front and rear tracks, and the abolition of super-sticky slick tyres. This had been a true revolution, one perhaps even more significant than the introduction of the stepped bottom in '95 that had provided the designers with much food for thought. The '98 season saw cars that were very different to one another, but more importantly during the year drastic modifications were made to previously untouchable parameters such as the wheelbase and weight distribution on almost all the cars, with the exception of the McLarens of course. As a consequence the following season that drew to a close at Suzuka on the 31st of October proved to some extent to be a consolidation of trends that had emerged a year earlier. The fundamental parameters in the design of the cars settled around the values adopted the previous season with only two teams, Minardi and Jordan, modifying their wheelbase dimensions (it should, moreover, be pointed out that in the case of the Irish team, only the undecided Damon Hill's car was altered and only for the last few races of the season). Ferrari's conquest of the constructors' trophy after a barren patch that had lasted from 1983, rewarded the reliability and consistency of the F399 in a season influenced by factors beyond the realm of pure performance. We are referring here to Michael Schumacher's dramatic crash at Silverstone and his subsequent enforced absence from no less than 6 Grands Prix, and to the sequence of unforced errors committed by McLaren. This anomalous situation allowed Eddie Irvine to find himself leading the drivers' championship

from Mika Hakkinen going into the last race at Suzuka. This was also the season that saw the consacration of two emergent teams, Jordan Mugen Honda and Stewart Ford. With 3 victories between them, they broke the Ferrari-McLaren hegemony and finished third and fourth in the constructors' championship ahead of the more highly fancied Williams and Benetton who both suffered second successive seasons in the doldrums.

Once again Maranello produced a car that at the start of the season was outclassed performance-wise by the McLaren but which recovered well, thanks largely to greater reliability and more favourable tuning and handling characteristics. The F399 immediately proved to be an extremely well balanced car, easier to set-up and drive than its predecessors. Deriving from the experience garnered over the previous season with the F300, especially with regards to the wheelbase dimension, the '99 car retained its predecessor's high nose and general layout. Ferrari's aerodynamics once again appeared to be an inferior to those of the McLaren, with greater turbulence in the delicate Coke-bottle area. This aspect was modified on the occasion of the French GP, something of a tradition with Maranello's cars. Less extreme and further from the cutting-edge in technical terms than its rival the MP4/14, the F399's superior reliability and its user-friendly nature translated into a considerable advantage on those tracks with less reference parameters. The marque's return to championship success coincided with the reappearance of arrow-head (more properly trapezoidal) wings in the German GP, a curious throw-back to the aerodynamics of the glorious 70s cars. Michael Schumacher's re-entry was marked by the introduction of new techni-

Jordan 199

Williams FW21

Benetton B199

cal features in the field of aerodynamics. Features that were to create an outcry in the successive Malaysian GP. The premature disqualification of the Ferraris for the presumed irregularity of the projection of the curved upper part of the barge board was later dismissed after more accurate measurement of the component revealed that it was within the permitted tolerance.

The 1998 championship saw Ferrari engaged in a rather less breathless chase to catch up with the McLarens. The three sectors that saw the most development were those of the engine, the aerodynamics and the suspension. In the first, the introduction of the two evolutions, the 048 B and C, was very well judged, in contrast with previous strategies in which evolution steps were perhaps used only in practice and not always successfully. Slightly heavier and bulkier than the Mercedes 10-cylinder, the Ferrari unit prevailed over its rival in terms of reliability, drivebility and greater ease of installation. The electro-hydraulic problems suffered by the MP4/14 early in the season were largely due to the greater vibration deriving from the latest engine produced by Mario Illien.

For the second successive season McLaren produced the championship's most competitive and fastest car, the MP4/14, and yet Ron Dennis' team missed out on the Constructors' Championship due to a series of tactical errors and, above all, because the second car designed at Woking by Adrian Newey was more unreliable and critical to set-up and drive. In order to cure the car's unruly track manners numerous experiments were carried out such as those involving a longer wheelbase and high exhausts, features which were never actually used in the races. After taking a year to settle in at McLaren, the father of the last World Championship winning Williams gave free rein to his imagination and designed an extremely innovative car that contained few compromises. The MP4/14's technical superiority was, however, largely negated by its unreliability, Coulthard's on-track faux pas and a number of incidents involving Hakkinen such as the wheel lost at Silverstone and the rear tyre exploded at the German GP. An obvious example of the technical extremes to which Newey went were the barge boards behind the front wheels. In order to save weight and improve torsional rigidity a high price was paid in terms of practicality: about an hour was needed to replace the components against at most five minutes for the other cars. The extremely light and compact Mercedes V-10 designed by Mario Illien was a perfect match for the Newey philosophy, allowing him to increase ballast to no less than 70 kg and thus vary weight distribution as and when necessary.

The '99 season saw the confirmation of two new technical features that emerged in 1998 and were destined for widespread adoption. These were the central positioning of the oil reservoir within the fuel tank and the large-scale use of ballast to modify weight distribution and add a further variable in the search for optimal set-ups according to the characteristics of the individual circuits. While in 1998 only 3 teams (Stewart, Arrows and Prost) abandoned the classic oil reservoir location between engine and gearbox, no less than 8 adopted the central location in '99 (with McLaren, Jordan, Benetton, Minardi and BAR joining the pioneers) and it would not be unreasonable to assume that the new layout will become universal in the 2000 season. As

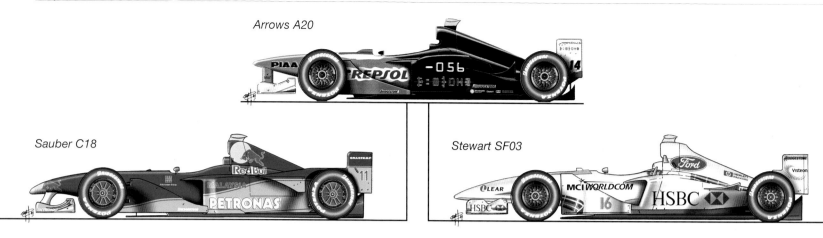

*Arrows A20*

*Sauber C18*

*Stewart SF03*

for ballast, the designers managed to bring their cars in at up to 70 kg under the minimum weight allowing the sidepods and driving position to be set further back, clearly favouring the aerodynamic package whilst maintaining a weight distribution with around 43-45% bearing on the front axle to overcome the chronic understeer provoked by the grooved tyres. Tyre efficiency was penalised by the addition of a fourth groove at the front, further reducing the total contact patch area, and by the use of harder compounds than in 1998.

Jordan established itself as the championship's third force thanks to Heinz Harald Frentzen's two victories and was even in the running for the title up to the third-last race at the Nürburgring. Mike Gascoyne's car inherited the excellent work of Gary Anderson who, at the end of the '98 season, had moved on to Stewart. The 199 was the car with the smallest frontal area thanks to an extreme interpretation of the lateral structures protecting the driver, almost completely replaced by the false structural fins introduced by Williams in '96. The Jordan was also the only car without a fully load-bearing engine although its anchorage was stiffened by two arms locking onto the cylinder heads. Much of the credit for this car's performance was due to the constant development of the Mugen Honda 10-cylinder engine, culminating in two separate qualifying and race evolutions at Suzuka.
The '99 season saw the definitive emergence of the Stewart team which won its first Grand Prix with Johnny Herbert at the Nürburgring. The SF03, once again designed under the direction of Alan Jenkins and revised and corrected by Gary Anderson, made an impact from the earliest races. This was the '99 car that was most strongly influenced by the fea-

tures introduced by McLaren in 1998, both in terms of aerodynamics and general layout. On the other hand, Jenkins has the merit of having been the first to move the oil reservoir from between engine and gearbox to a location within the fuel tank adopted by no less than 8 teams in '99 including McLaren. The symbiosis between Ford and the small Scottish team became increasingly significant after it was bought out by the automotive giant. The new 10-cylinder engine was designed according to revolutionary criteria with the aim of reducing weight and size. While the unit proved to be very fragile with 4 failures, a negative record beaten only by the Peugeot with 5, it did open the way for the design of ultra-lightweight engines that were virtually disposable after each race, the better to integrate with the constructional philosophy of underweight cars.

It was clear that in 1999 Williams had yet to get over the loss of the genial Adrian Newey and for the second year running the team failed to win a race, falling from third to fifth overall in the Constructors' Championship. The Gavin Fisher and Geoff Willis (an aerodynamicist) duo's car was the most individual design but also the one subjected to the most modification during the season. It was the only car with very low sidepods and exhausts blowing in the central tunnel area, with two different layouts used before the lateral exhaust location was adopted from the British GP, together with new bodywork with further modifications to the area in front of the rear wheels at the Austrian GP and the successive race in Hungary. Williams reintroduced cast-iron brakes to Formula 1 (with a consequent increase in unsprung weight of around 9 kg), both to satisfy the demands of Alessandro Zanardi and to try to overcome the problem of low operating

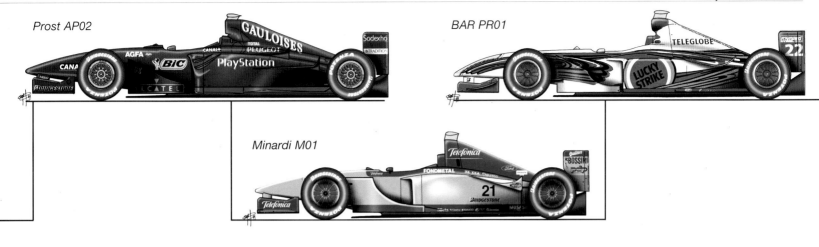

Prost AP02

BAR PR01

Minardi M01

temperatures on the tyres. Patrick Head's team was the most successful of those using the Supertec 10-cylinder.

The three teams that had been nurturing ambitions of joining the big league, Benetton, Sauber and Prost, suffered a frustrating season. The most disappointing was Benetton which paid a high price for the risky decision to use a differential for the front brakes that entailed a considerable weight handicap and elongated the wheelbase to an absurd degree. Close behind was the bulky and hardly competitive Prost AP02 while the Sauber was betrayed by the chronic fragility of its gearbox (7 breakages) and no less than 12 accidents. Arrows was the only team to use its 1998 car (with the wheelbase extended at the front) and scored just one championship point, as did Minardi. The M01 designed by Gustav Brunner's staff featured a brand-new rear suspension layout with horizontal torsion bars and vertical dampers but its aerodynamic package and the 10-cylinder Ford used by Stewart in '98 appeared to have reached a development ceiling.

The 1999 season was the first without the prestigious Tyrrell name after almost 30 years, its place being taken by the ambitious BAR outfit led by the '97 world champion Jacques Villeneuve. Much may be forgiven a debutante, but the first car produced by Reynard for BAR outdid even the most pessimistic predictions in terms of unreliability and fragility, and this in spite of a design with no particularly innovative features. Two statistics sum up the team's year: 18 mechanical failures and 6 accidents. Talking about accidents, the two safety-related innovations introduced by the Federation for the 1999 season, the wheel ties and the

extractable driver's seat, were not wholly convincing. In certain cases the first proved to have a boomerang effect with wheels being trapped against the sides of the monocoque and eventually acting as a kind of band-saw as in part happened in the two crashes in which drivers were injured, Zonta with the BAR in Brazil and Schumacher with the Ferrari at Silverstone. As for the extractable seat, the various methods of attaching it to the chassis adopted by the different teams frequently made rescue operations even more difficult, obliging the Federation to specify standard anchorages for all cockpits. Still on the subject of safety, the breakage of the roll bar on Diniz's Sauber which overturned at around 90 kph at the first corner of the GP of Europe was the classic last straw that persuaded the authorities to tighten up the crash test norms for these structures in the 2000 season.

The analysis of the season retains a thematic subdivision so as to highlight specific aspects of the various cars. This structure may in certain cases overlap the chapters relating to the evolution of the individual cars but will help in providing direct comparisons of the different solutions adopted.
The creation of the tables detailing «Cars» and «Engines» was the fruit of painstaking cross-referenced research conducted with the various designers towards the end of the season so as to overcome the problem of what are frequently approximate data provided by the teams at the launch of new cars.

As the fields lacking official data were ever more numerous, in the case of the «Engines» table we once again called on Ingegner Enrico Benzing to provide estimated figures.

# Chassis HISTORY

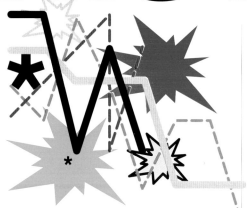

The diagrams detailing the chassis used by the various teams that traditionally introduce this volume provide a technical interpretation of the Formula 1 season. In 1999 there were no major revolutions such as chassis being lightened or modified during the season as had happened in 1997. After a season like that of '98, characterised by a host of chassis written off in a single multiple pile-up at the start of the Belgian GP (4 chassis destroyed and damaged, with a total of 8 being written off completely); in 1999 this number dropped to 6. Unfortunately, in contrast with '98 damage was not restricted to the cars. The most serious accident was Schumacher's in the early stages of British GP at Silverstone which had serious consequences for the German driver who was obliged to miss 6 races after breaking his right leg. Earlier in the season the young Ricardo Zonta had also had to miss three races due to fractures sustained when he crashed during practice for the Brazilian GP. Spa was once again a low point of Jacques Villeneuve's season as, like the previous year, he was involved in a frightening accident during prac-

tice, immediately imitated by his team-mate Zonta. The outcome was one chassis destroyed and a second badly damaged. The debutante BAR team's performance over the season failed to live to expectations due to a series of accidents and mechanical failures, as the chassis table in part reveals. BAR was the first team to write off a chassis (in Zonta's accident at the second race in Brazil) and also finished with the record number of chassis destroyed (2) and damaged (4). The last chassis to be written off was Diniz's Sauber at the GP of Europe. Looking at the number of chassis destroyed, FIA's new normative obliging wheels to be anchored by cables appears suspect. In both Schumacher and Zonta's accidents the wheel trapped against the chassis eventually cut into it. The total number of teams remained at 11 with BAR replacing the glorious Tyrrell which withdrew at the end of the '98 season.

# MC LAREN • *MP4/14* • Nos 1-2

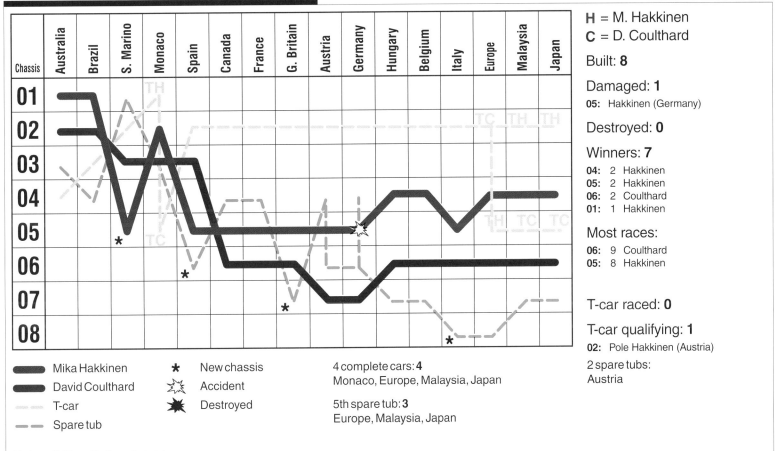

H = M. Hakkinen
C = D. Coulthard

Built: **8**

Damaged: **1**
**05:** Hakkinen (Germany)

Destroyed: **0**

Winners: **7**
**04:** 2 Hakkinen
**05:** 2 Hakkinen
**06:** 2 Coulthard
**01:** 1 Hakkinen

Most races:
**06:** 9 Coulthard
**05:** 8 Hakkinen

T-car raced: **0**

T-car qualifying: **1**
**02:** Pole Hakkinen (Austria)

2 spare tubs:
Austria

Legend:
Mika Hakkinen
David Coulthard
- - - T-car
— — Spare tub

* New chassis
Accident
Destroyed

4 complete cars: **4**
Monaco, Europe, Malaysia, Japan

5th spare tub: **3**
Europe, Malaysia, Japan

**Note valid for all chassis tables:**
The initials with drivers' colours, inserted in the drawings, refer to the use of the T-car in the G.P. corresponding to the box. The drivers' initials in the colour of the T with which it is combined, instead refers to the use of two assembled T-cars.

## FACTS AND FIGURES

The maximum number of chassis constructed during the season dropped by one. Ferrari had previously held the record of 9 tubs built in a season, while in '99 it constructed 8, as did McLaren and BAR, followed by Benetton, Sauber and Prost with 7, Williams, Jordan and Stewart with 6 and Minardi with just 4.

McLaren's chassis no. 8 debuted as the spare tub at the Italian GP but was never assembled, even though McLaren made the effort to prepare no less than 4 complete cars for its 2 drivers for the last 3 races, as did Ferrari for the last 2 races in Asia.

Ferrari never took the last of the F399 series, chassis no. 197, to the races, reserving it for private testing as shown in the table relating to the team from Maranello.

Arrows took part in the 1999 edition of the championship with modified versions of its '98 cars and thus built no new chassis. The team simply adapted 4 of the 7 tubs built in '98 to the new specifications. The diagram in fact lacks chassis nos. 1 and 3, the first destroyed in the pre-season crash test, the second in Salo's accident at the '98 Canadian GP. Chassis no. 06 was never used during the GP weekends despite being modified

BAR was the only team to race (with Zonta in the Belgian GP) one of the two cars destined for the subsequent private testing at Monza, following its two drivers' crashes in practice. Curiously, the same thing happened to Williams the previous season again at Spa and again following a practice accident involving Villeneuve. In '99 the Canadian started with the T-car which was in turn replaced by the spare tub assembled for the occasion.

The most successful chassis was Irvine's Ferrari no. 191 with three wins, followed by Schumacher's no. 193, Hakkinen's McLarens nos. 04 and 05, Coulthard's McLaren no. 06 and Frentzen's Jordan no. 05 with 2 wins each. Herbert's Stewart no. 03 won the remaining race.

The team that raced their T-car most frequently was Williams with 4 outings (Zanardi 3 and Schumacher 1), followed by Benetton and Minardi with 3 (Fisichella and Badoer 2, Wurz and Gene 1) and Stewart with 2 (Barrichello and Herbert once each). Prost and BAR used their T-cars once each with Panis and Villeneuve respectively. Only Ferrari and McLaren never had to race their T-cars.

The chassis that took part in the most GPs was the Minardi no. 01 that started every race, 15 with Badoer and 1 with Sarrazin,

# FERRARI • *F399* • Nos 3-4

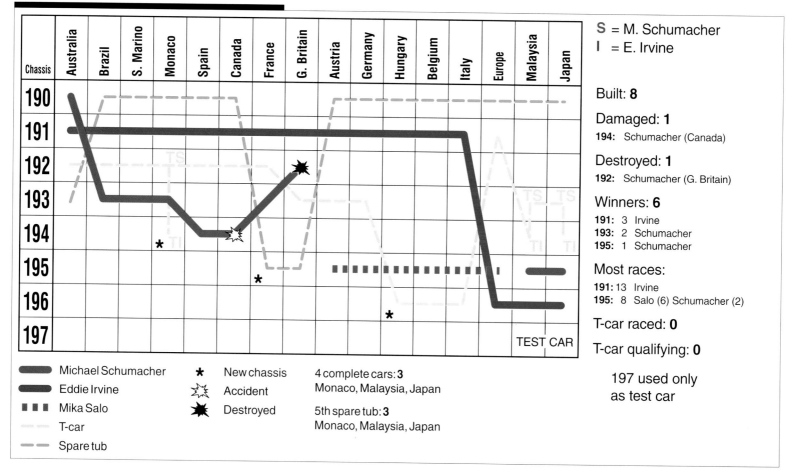

S = M. Schumacher
I = E. Irvine

**Built: 8**

**Damaged: 1**
194: Schumacher (Canada)

**Destroyed: 1**
192: Schumacher (G. Britain)

**Winners: 6**
191: 3 Irvine
193: 2 Schumacher
195: 1 Schumacher

**Most races:**
191: 13 Irvine
195: 8 Salo (6) Schumacher (2)

**T-car raced: 0**

**T-car qualifying: 0**

197 used only
as test car

| | |
|---|---|
| ━━ Michael Schumacher | ✳ New chassis |
| ━━ Eddie Irvine | ✸ Accident |
| ▪▪▪ Mika Salo | ✸ Destroyed |
| – – – T-car | |
| — — Spare tub | |

4 complete cars: **3**
Monaco, Malaysia, Japan

5th spare tub: **3**
Monaco, Malaysia, Japan

his replacement in Brazil. Hill's Jordan 04 and Barrichello's Stewart 04 raced 15 times while Gene's Minardi 04 started 14 races. Irvine's Ferrari no. 191 and Zanardi's Williams 05 both started 13 GPs. There were 12 races for Herbert's Stewart O5, and Panis's Prost 05, 11 for Wurz's Benetton 05 and Takagi's Arrows 02. Four chassis started 10 races: Frentzen's Jordan 05, Fisichella's Benetton 07, De La Rosa's Arrows 04 and Trulli's Prost 07. Those with 9 starts were: the Sauber no. 05 (6 with Diniz, 3 with Alesi) and the McLaren no. 06 with Coulthard. Those with 8 starts were: Hakkinen's McLaren 05, Schumacher's Williams 06 and the Bar no. 06 (4 Villeneuve, 3 Zonta, 1 Salo).

Fisichella's Benetton no. 07 was the unluckiest chassis: it was damaged by fans while stationary at the end of the Italian GP. Quickly repaired, it completed the season.

All the teams with the exception of Arrows and Minardi prepared 4 complete cars for Monaco. The exploit was repeated by McLaren at the GP of Europe, in Malaysia and Japan and by Ferrari in Malaysia and Japan only. These 2 teams brought their 5th spare chassis on 3 occasions: Ferrari at the Monaco, Malaysian and Japanese GPs, McLaren at the GP of Europe and the Malaysian and Japanese GPs.

As soon as they were available all the teams brought their 4th spare chassis (as shown in the diagram) to assemble in case of necessity. Jordan and Arrows left them behind at the British GP, their factories being very close to Silverstone.

The most reliable car was the Ferrari which completed no less than 1,857 of the 2000 laps in each GP, corresponding to 93%, followed by McLaren at 1,566 laps or 78%. This can easily be seen in the table which records, in order, the laps completed in each race, the finishes, the technical problems encountered during the races (the most frequent being highlighted), the accidents and the number of km and private testing days completed during the season.

| Chassis | 190 | 191 | 192 ✸ | 193 | 194 ✸ | 195 | 196 | 197 |
|---|---|---|---|---|---|---|---|---|
| First run | 03-02-99 | 22-02-99 | 01-03-99 | 02-04-99 | 14-05-99 | 16-06-99 | 15-08-99 | 19-10-99 |
| Km completed | 11.667,227 | 10.812,553 | 4.145,486 | 7.125,546 | 6.439,108 | 7.118,922 | 3.633,05 | 1.006,122 |

# WILLIAMS • *FW21* • Nos 5-6

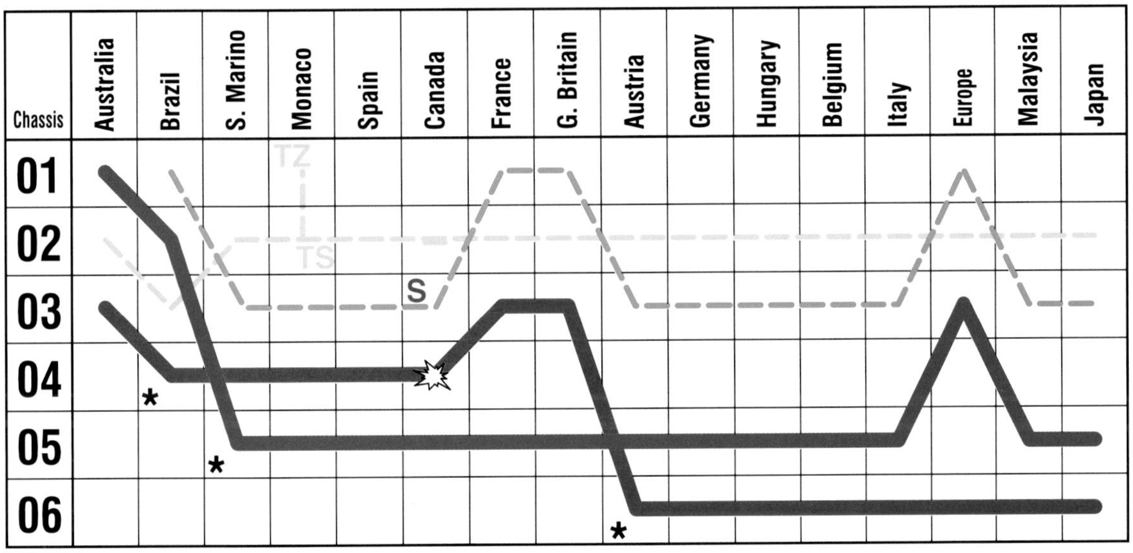


Alessandro Zanardi
Ralph Schumacher
T-car
Spare tub

★ New chassis
Accident
Destroyed

4 complete cars: 1
Monaco

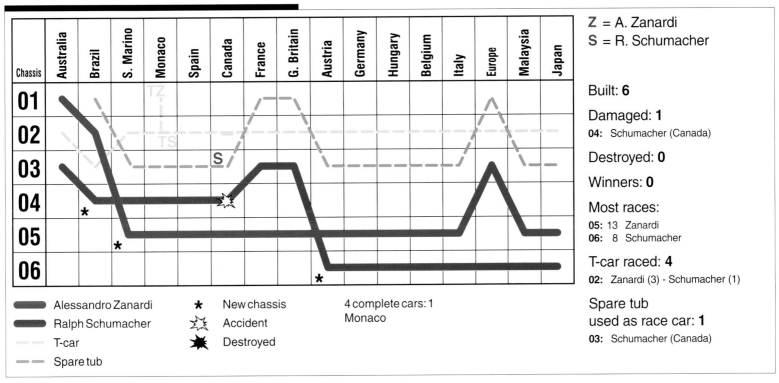

**Z** = A. Zanardi
**S** = R. Schumacher

Built: **6**

Damaged: **1**
**04:** Schumacher (Canada)

Destroyed: **0**

Winners: **0**

Most races:
**05:** 13 Zanardi
**06:** 8 Schumacher

T-car raced: **4**
**02:** Zanardi (3) - Schumacher (1)

Spare tub
used as race car: **1**
**03:** Schumacher (Canada)

# JORDAN • *199* • Nos 7-8

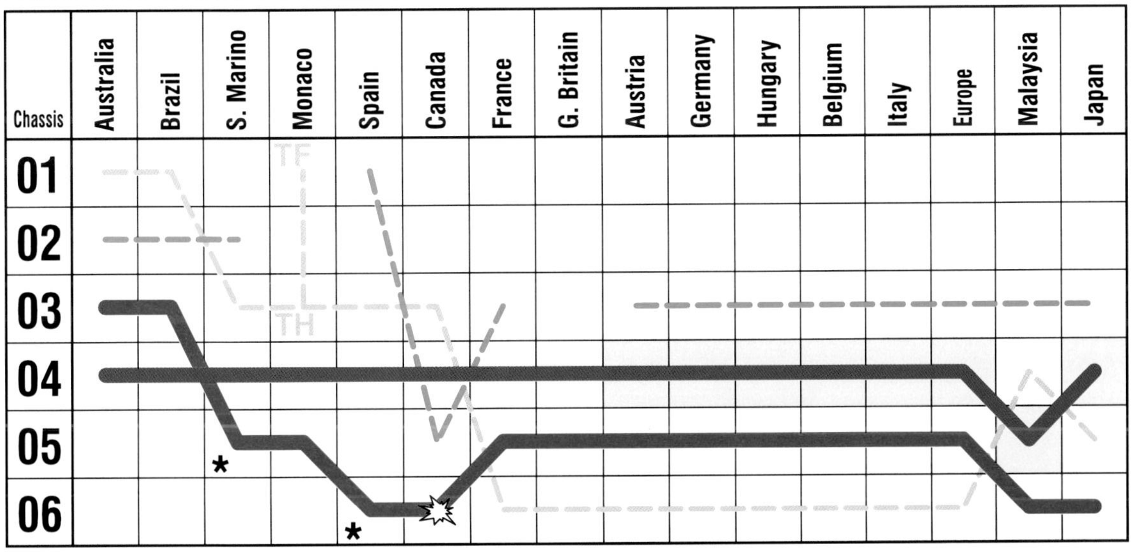


Damon Hill
Heinz Harald Frentzen
T-car
Spare tub

★ New chassis
Accident
Destroyed

4 complete cars: **1**
Monaco

No spare tub: **2**
Monaco, G. Britain

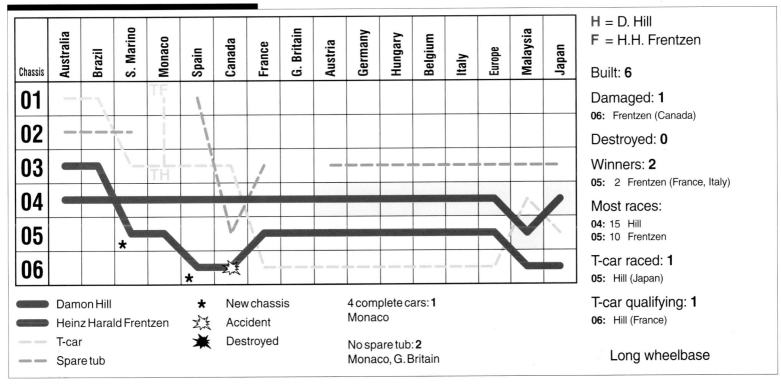

**H** = D. Hill
**F** = H.H. Frentzen

Built: **6**

Damaged: **1**
**06:** Frentzen (Canada)

Destroyed: **0**

Winners: **2**
**05:** 2 Frentzen (France, Italy)

Most races:
**04:** 15 Hill
**05:** 10 Frentzen

T-car raced: **1**
**05:** Hill (Japan)

T-car qualifying: **1**
**06:** Hill (France)

Long wheelbase

# BENETTON • *B199* • N<sub>os</sub> 9-10

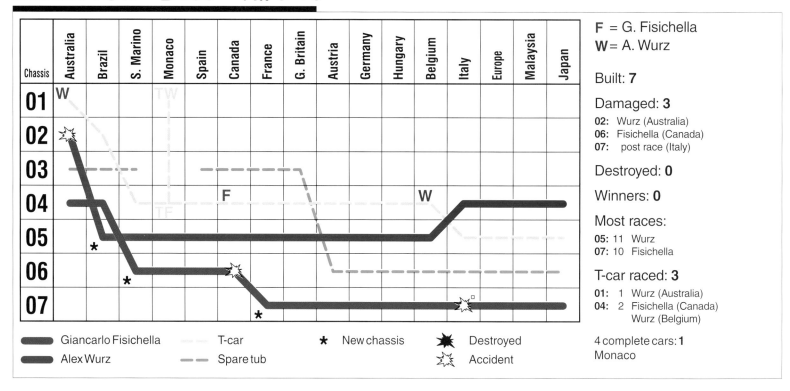

**F** = G. Fisichella
**W** = A. Wurz

Built: **7**

Damaged: **3**
**02:** Wurz (Australia)
**06:** Fisichella (Canada)
**07:** post race (Italy)

Destroyed: **0**

Winners: **0**

Most races:
**05:** 11 Wurz
**07:** 10 Fisichella

T-car raced: **3**
**01:** 1 Wurz (Australia)
**04:** 2 Fisichella (Canada)
        Wurz (Belgium)

4 complete cars: **1**
Monaco

Legend:
- Giancarlo Fisichella
- Alex Wurz
- T-car
- Spare tub
- * New chassis
- Destroyed
- Accident

# SAUBER • *C18* • N<sub>os</sub> 11-12

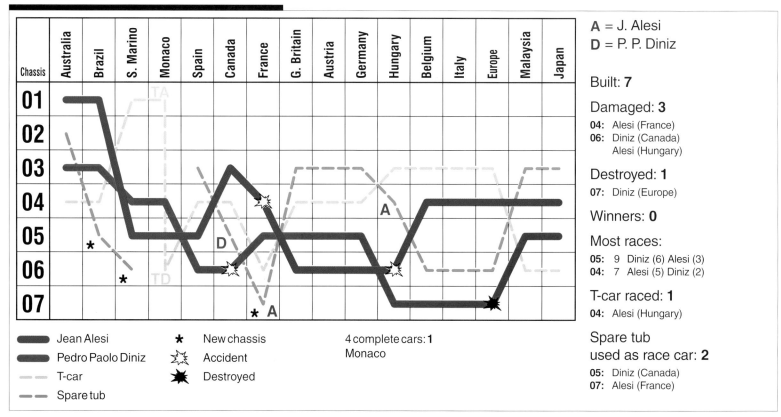

**A** = J. Alesi
**D** = P. P. Diniz

Built: **7**

Damaged: **3**
**04:** Alesi (France)
**06:** Diniz (Canada)
        Alesi (Hungary)

Destroyed: **1**
**07:** Diniz (Europe)

Winners: **0**

Most races:
**05:** 9 Diniz (6) Alesi (3)
**04:** 7 Alesi (5) Diniz (2)

T-car raced: **1**
**04:** Alesi (Hungary)

Spare tub
used as race car: **2**
**05:** Diniz (Canada)
**07:** Alesi (France)

Legend:
- Jean Alesi
- Pedro Paolo Diniz
- T-car
- Spare tub
- * New chassis
- Accident
- Destroyed

4 complete cars: **1**
Monaco

# ARROWS • *A20* • N<sub>os</sub> 14-15

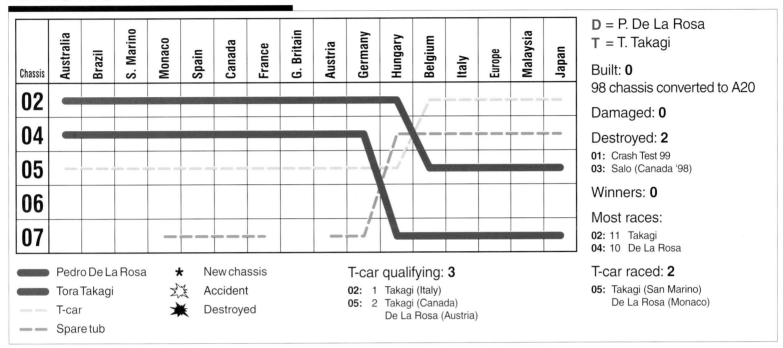

| Chassis | Australia | Brazil | S. Marino | Monaco | Spain | Canada | France | G. Britain | Austria | Germany | Hungary | Belgium | Italy | Europe | Malaysia | Japan |
|---|---|---|---|---|---|---|---|---|---|---|---|---|---|---|---|---|
| 02 | | | | | | | | | | | | | | | | |
| 04 | | | | | | | | | | | | | | | | |
| 05 | | | | | | | | | | | | | | | | |
| 06 | | | | | | | | | | | | | | | | |
| 07 | | | | | | | | | | | | | | | | |

**Legend:**
- ━━━ Pedro De La Rosa
- ━━━ Tora Takagi
- ─ ─ T-car
- ━ ━ Spare tub
- ✴ New chassis
- ✴ Accident
- ✹ Destroyed

**T-car qualifying: 3**
- 02: 1 Takagi (Italy)
- 05: 2 Takagi (Canada)
- De La Rosa (Austria)

**D** = P. De La Rosa
**T** = T. Takagi

Built: **0**
98 chassis converted to A20

Damaged: **0**

Destroyed: **2**
- 01: Crash Test 99
- 03: Salo (Canada '98)

Winners: **0**

Most races:
- 02: 11 Takagi
- 04: 10 De La Rosa

T-car raced: **2**
- 05: Takagi (San Marino)
- De La Rosa (Monaco)

# STEWART • *SF03* • N<sub>os</sub> 16-17

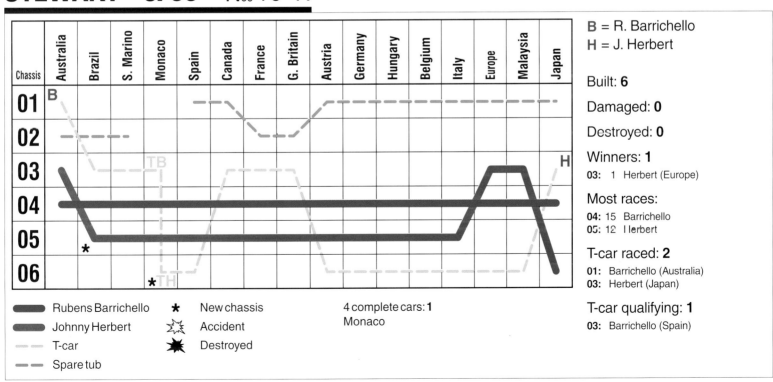

| Chassis | Australia | Brazil | S. Marino | Monaco | Spain | Canada | France | G. Britain | Austria | Germany | Hungary | Belgium | Italy | Europe | Malaysia | Japan |
|---|---|---|---|---|---|---|---|---|---|---|---|---|---|---|---|---|
| 01 | B | | | | | | | | | | | | | | | |
| 02 | | | | | | | | | | | | | | | | |
| 03 | | | | | | | | | | | | | | | | H |
| 04 | | | | | | | | | | | | | | | | |
| 05 | | ✴ | | | | | | | | | | | | | | |
| 06 | | | | ✴ | | | | | | | | | | | | |

**Legend:**
- ━━━ Rubens Barrichello
- ━━━ Johnny Herbert
- ─ ─ T-car
- ━ ━ Spare tub
- ✴ New chassis
- ✴ Accident
- ✹ Destroyed

**4 complete cars: 1**
Monaco

**B** = R. Barrichello
**H** = J. Herbert

Built: **6**

Damaged: **0**

Destroyed: **0**

Winners: **1**
- 03: 1 Herbert (Europe)

Most races:
- 04: 15 Barrichello
- 05: 12 Herbert

T-car raced: **2**
- 01: Barrichello (Australia)
- 03: Herbert (Japan)

T-car qualifying: **1**
- 03: Barrichello (Spain)

# PROST • *AP02* • N<sub>os</sub> 18-19

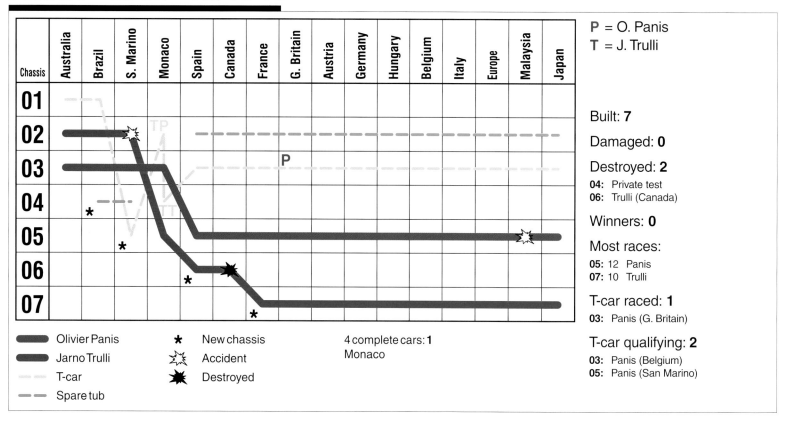

P = O. Panis
T = J. Trulli

Built: **7**

Damaged: **0**

Destroyed: **2**
**04:** Private test
**06:** Trulli (Canada)

Winners: **0**

Most races:
**05:** 12 Panis
**07:** 10 Trulli

T-car raced: **1**
**03:** Panis (G. Britain)

T-car qualifying: **2**
**03:** Panis (Belgium)
**05:** Panis (San Marino)

Legend:
- ▬▬▬ Olivier Panis
- ▬▬▬ Jarno Trulli
- – – – T-car
- — — Spare tub
- ✳ New chassis
- 💥 Accident
- ✸ Destroyed

4 complete cars: **1**
Monaco

# MINARDI • *M01* • N<sub>os</sub> 20-21

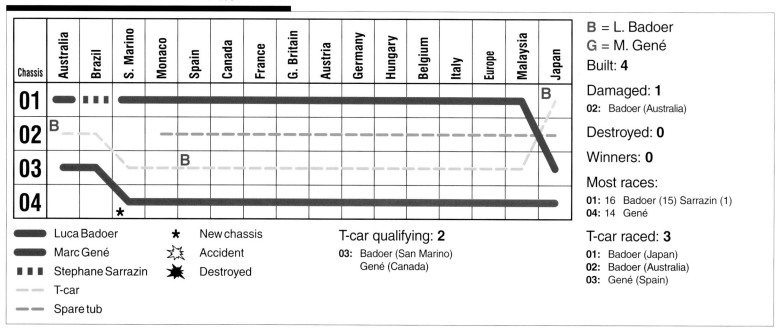

B = L. Badoer
G = M. Gené

Built: **4**

Damaged: **1**
**02:** Badoer (Australia)

Destroyed: **0**

Winners: **0**

Most races:
**01:** 16 Badoer (15) Sarrazin (1)
**04:** 14 Gené

T-car raced: **3**
**01:** Badoer (Japan)
**02:** Badoer (Australia)
**03:** Gené (Spain)

Legend:
- ▬▬▬ Luca Badoer
- ▬▬▬ Marc Gené
- ▪▪▪ Stephane Sarrazin
- – – – T-car
- — — Spare tub
- ✳ New chassis
- 💥 Accident
- ✸ Destroyed

T-car qualifying: **2**
**03:** Badoer (San Marino)
Gené (Canada)

# BAR • *PR01* • Nos 22-23

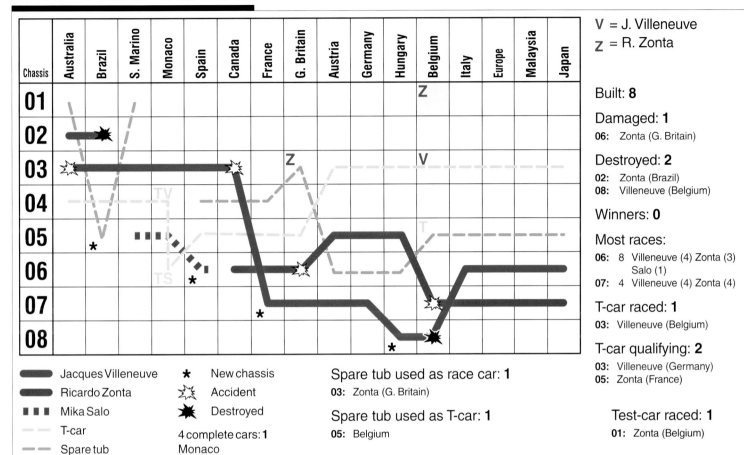

V = J. Villeneuve
Z = R. Zonta

**Built: 8**

**Damaged: 1**
06: Zonta (G. Britain)

**Destroyed: 2**
02: Zonta (Brazil)
08: Villeneuve (Belgium)

**Winners: 0**

**Most races:**
06: 8 Villeneuve (4) Zonta (3)
Salo (1)
07: 4 Villeneuve (4) Zonta (4)

**T-car raced: 1**
03: Villeneuve (Belgium)

**T-car qualifying: 2**
03: Villeneuve (Germany)
05: Zonta (France)

**Test-car raced: 1**
01: Zonta (Belgium)

━━━ Jacques Villeneuve
━━━ Ricardo Zonta
▪▪▪ Mika Salo
--- T-car
--- Spare tub

★ New chassis
✲ Accident
✸ Destroyed
4 complete cars: 1
Monaco

**Spare tub used as race car: 1**
03: Zonta (G. Britain)

**Spare tub used as T-car: 1**
05: Belgium

| | laps completed (%) | finishes* | technical failures | accidents | test km | days |
|---|---|---|---|---|---|---|
| **Ferrari** | **1857 (93 %)** | **28** | **2 - engine (1), brake (1)** | **2** | **30291** | **96** |
| **McLaren** | 1566 (78 %) | 20 | 9 - gearbox (3) | 3 | 26314 | 64 |
| **Stewart** | 1552 (78 %) | 18 | 12 - engine (4) | 2 | 15422 | 47 |
| **Benetton** | 1472 (74 %) | 17 | 8 - engine (2), drive-shaft (2) | 7 | 20787 | 54 |
| **Jordan** | 1436 (72 %) | 19 | 6 - electrical (3) | 6** | 17317 | 44 |
| **Williams** | 1413 (71 %) | 15 | 8 - differential (4) | 7 | 19088 | 54 |
| **Minardi** | 1402 (70 %) | 16 | 9 - gearbox (5) | 7 | 6873 | 31 |
| **Prost** | 1399 (70 %) | 18 | 11 - engine (5) | 3 | 21622 | 61 |
| **Arrows** | 1269 (63 %) | 10 | 17 - gearbox (8) | 5 | 6720 | 31 |
| **BAR** | 1234 (62 %) | 8 | 18 - clutch (5) | 6 | 11304 | 45 |
| **Sauber** | 1207 (60 %) | 11 | 9 - gearbox (7) | 12 | 16949 | 51 |

\* Each team had 32 starts.
\*\* Hill gave up in Japan, so it was neither a technical failure nor an accident.

# Table of CARS

| | 1 - 2 McLAREN | 3 - 4 FERRARI | 5 - 6 WILLIAMS | 7 - 8 JORDAN | 9 - 10 BENETTON |
|---|---|---|---|---|---|
| **CAR** | **MP4/14** | **F 399** | **FW 21** | **199** | **B 199** |
| Designers | Adrian Newey<br>Neil Oatley | Ross Brawn<br>Rory Byrne | Patrick Head<br>Gavin Fisher - Geoff Willis | Mike Gascoyne | Pat Symons<br>Nick Wirth |
| Race engineers | Steve Hallam<br>Mark Slade (1) - Pat Fry (2) | Ignazio Lunetta - Carlo Cantoni[b] (3) - Luca Baldisserri (4) | Greg Wheeler - John Russel[c] (5) - Craig Wilson (6) | Dino Toso (7) - Sam Michael[f] - Tim Holloway (8) | Alan Permain - Marc Heard (9)<br>Christian Silk - Rod Nelson (10) |
| Chief mechanic | Mike Negline | Nigel Stepney | Carl Gaden | Tim Edwards | Mick Ainsley - Cowlishawl |

## CHASSIS

| | MP4/14 | F 399 | FW 21 | 199 | B 199 |
|---|---|---|---|---|---|
| Wheelbase | 3020-3100[a] mm* | 3052 mm* | 3070 mm* | 3050-3114[g] mm | 3285 mm* |
| Front track | 1490 mm* | 1490 mm | 1460 mm | 1500 mm | 1490 mm |
| Rear track | 1425 mm* | 1405 mm | 1405 mm | 1418 mm | 1405 mm |
| Front suspension** | 2+1 dampers and torsion bars | 2+1 dampers and torsion bars | 2+1 dampers and torsion bars | 2+1 dampers | 2+1 dampers and torsion bars |
| Rear suspension** | 2+1 dampers and torsion bars | 2+1 dampers and torsion bars | 2 dampers[d] | 2+1 dampers | 2 dampers |
| Dampers | McLaren-Penske | Sachs | Williams-Penske | Penske | Dynamic Suspensions |
| Brake calipers | A+P | Brembo | A+P | Brembo | Brembo |
| Brake discs | Hitco | Carbon Industrie | Carbon Industrie - Hitco[e] | Hitco - Carbon Industrie | Carbon Industrie |
| Wheels | Enkey | BBS | O.Z. | O.Z. | BBS |
| Radiators | Calsonic-Marston | Secan | Secan | Secan | Secan - Marston |
| Oil tank | Central location inside fuel tank | Between engine and gearbox | Between engine and gearbox | Central location inside fuel tank | Central location inside fuel tank |

## GEARBOX

| | | | | | |
|---|---|---|---|---|---|
| | Longitudinal magnesium | Longitudinal fabricated | Longitudinal magnesium | Longitudinal magnesium | Longitudinal magnesium |
| Gear selection | Semiautomatic 7 gears | Semiautomatic 7 gears | Semiautomatic 6 gears | Semiautomatic 6 gears | Semiautomatic 6 gears |
| Clutch | A+P | Sachs - A+P | A+P | Sachs | A+P |
| Pedals | 2 | 2 | 2 | 2 | 2 |

## ENGINE

| | | | | | |
|---|---|---|---|---|---|
| | Mercedes FO110/H | Ferrari 048 | Supertec FB 01 | Mugen Honda MF301-HD | Supertec FB 01 |
| Total capacity | 2996.0 cmc | 2996.6 cmc | 2996.6 cmc | 2998.4 cmc | 2996.6 cmc |
| No cylinders and V-angle | 10 - V 72° | 10 - V 80° | 10 - V 71° | 10 - V 72° | 10 - V 71° |
| Electronics | TAG Electronic | Magneti Marelli | Magneti Marelli | TAG Electronic | Magneti Marelli |
| Fuel | Mobil | Shell | Petrobras | Elf | Agip |
| Oil | Mobil | Shell | Castrol | Elf | Agip |
| Fuel tank capacity | 135 l* | 141 l* | 132 l* | 145 l* | 120 l |
| Dashboard | TAG Electronic | Magneti Marelli | Williams | Jordan | Benetton |

| 11 - 12 SAUBER | 14 - 15 ARROWS | 16 - 17 STEWART | 18 - 19 PROST | 20 - 21 MINARDI | 22 - 23 BAR |
|---|---|---|---|---|---|
| C 18 | A 20 | SF 03 | AP 02 | M 01 | PR 01 |
| Leo Ress | Mike Coughlan | Gary Anderson | Alan Jenkins[i] | Gustav Brunner / Gabriele Tredozi | Malcom Oastler / Andrew Green |
| Gabriele Delli Colli (11) - Steve Clark - Remy Decorzent[h] (12) | Nick Chester (14) / Chris Dyer (15) | Robin Gearing - Andy Miller (16) / Simon Smart - Andy Le Fleming (17) | Humprey Corbett (18) / Gilles Allegoet (19) | Gian Franco Fantuzzi (20) / J. François Sinteff (21) | Jock Clear (22) / Mick Cook (21) |
| Urs Kuratle | Stuart Cowle | Dave Redding | Alan Sauvagere | Gabriele Pagliarini | Alastair Gibson |
| 3100 mm | 3025 mm | 3035 mm* | 3242 mm* | 2950-3010 mm[l] | 3050 mm |
| 1480 mm | 1490 mm | 1490 mm | 1490 mm* | 1479 mm | 1450 mm |
| 1390 mm | 1405 mm | 1405 mm | 1405 mm* | 1421 mm | 1405 mm |
| 2+1 dampers and torsion bars | 2+1 dampers and torsion bars | 2+1 dampers and torsion bars | 2+1 dampers and torsion bars | 2 dampers and torsion bars | 2 dampers and torsion bars |
| 2+1 dampers and torsion bars | 2+1 dampers and torsion bars | 2+1 dampers | 2+1 dampers | 2 dampers and torsion bars | 2 dampers |
| Sachs | Dynamic Suspensions | Stewart - Penske | Dynamic Suspensions | Sachs | Koni |
| Brembo | A+P - Arrows | A+P | Brembo | Brembo | A+P |
| Carbon Industrie | Carbon Industrie | Carbon Industrie | Carbon Industrie | Carbon Industrie | Hitco - Carbon Industrie |
| O.Z. | BBS | BBS | BBS | Fondmetal | O.Z. |
| Calsonic | Secan | Secan | Secan | Secan | Marston |
| Between engine and gearbox | Central location inside fuel tank | Central location inside fuel tank | Central location inside fuel tank | Central location inside fuel tank | Central location inside fuel tank |
| Longitudinal magnesium | Longitudinal carbon | Longitudinal | Longitudinal | Longitudinal | Longitudinal alluminium |
| Semiautomatic 7 gears | Semiautomatic 6 gears | Semiautomatic 6 gears | Semiautomatic 6 gears | Semiautomatic 6 gears | Pneumatic 6 gears |
| Sachs | A+P | A+P | A+P | A+P | A+P |
| 3 | 2 | 2 | 2 | 2 | 2 |
| Petronas 047 03A/B | Arrows A20 | Ford Zetec CR-1 Ev3 | Peugeot A18 Ev 4/5 | Ford Zetec - R | Supertec FB 01 |
| 2998.3 cmc | 2998.1 cmc | 2998.0 cmc | 2998.3 cmc | 2998.3 cmc | 2996.6 cmc |
| 10 - V 80° | 10 - V 72° | 10 - V 72° | 10 - V 72° | 10 - V 72° | 10 - V 71° |
| Magneti Marelli | TAG Electronic | Ford - Visteon | TAG Electronic | Magneti Marelli | P.I. Magneti Marelli |
| Shell | Repsol | Texaco | Total | Elf | Elf |
| Shell | Repsol | Texaco | Total | Elf | Elf |
| 140 l | 135 l | 118 l* | 125 l | 145 l | 130 l |
| Magneti Marelli | Arrows - TAG | Stewart P.I. | Prost | Magneti Marelli | Bar P.I. |

**Variations during the season**

a) Long wheelbase never used during practice
b) Carlo Cantoni track engineer for Mika Salo
c) John Russell joined Greg Wheeler from the French GP
d) Third damper at the rear from the GP of Europe
e) Iron brakes used in practice for the Austrian GP
f) Tim Holloway track engineer for Frentzen, Austrian GP only
g) Long wheelbase used by Hill only from Austrian GP
h) Remy Decorzent replaced Steve Clark after the Hungarian GP
i) Alan Jenkins appointed after British GP
l) Long wheelbase introduced on Badoer's car only at Imola, subsequently on all the Minardi

\* extimated value

\*\* push-rod for all cars

# Table of ENGINES

| | MERCEDES | FERRARI | MUGEN-HONDA | FORD V10 |
|---|---|---|---|---|
| Type | ILMOR FO110H | 048 B<br>048 C | MF-301-HD | COSWORTH CR1 EV3/4 |
| Total cubic capacity | 2996.0 cmc | 2998.3 cmc<br>2996.6 cmc | 2998.4 cmc | 2998.0 cmc |
| No cylinders and V-angle | 10 - V 72° | 10 - V 80° | 10 - V 72° | 10 - V 72° |
| Bore and stroke (mm) | 93.00 x 44.11* | 95.00 x 42.30*<br>96.00 x 41.40* | 93.00 x 44.14* | 93.00 x 44.13* |
| Compression ratio | 13.3 : 1* | 13.2 : 1* | 13.2 : 1* | 13.2 : 1* |
| Number of valves and return system | 4 pneumatic | 4 pneumatic | 4 pneumatic | 4 pneumatic |
| Maximum revs | 17.100* (Q 17.400)* | 17.100* (Q 17.500)*<br>17.300* (Q 17.700)* | 16.800* (Q 17.200)* | 17.000 (Q 17.500) |
| Maximum power | 800 CV* (Q 815 CV)* | 780 CV* (Q 795 CV)*<br>790 CV* (Q 805 CV)* | 780 CV* (Q 790 CV)* | 775 CV (Q 785 CV)* |
| Bearings | 6 | 6 | 6 | 6 |
| Induction system | Moving trumpets | Moving trumpets | Fixed | Fixed |
| Throttle | Electronic-Barrel | Electro-Hydraulic | Electro-Hydraulic | Electro-Hydraulic |
| Electronics | TAG - Electr. Sys 2000 | Magneti Marelli | Honda PGM-FI/IG | Ford Visteon VCS |
| Block | Aluminium | Aluminium | Light alloy | Aluminium alloy |
| Length | 590 mm | 618 mm<br>609 mm | 625 mm | 569 mm |
| Width | 546 mm | 538 mm<br>530 mm | 520 mm | 506 mm |
| Height | 476 mm | 396 mm<br>378 mm | 450 mm | 485 mm<br>375 mm |
| Weight | 100 kg | 114 kg | 110 kg | 99 kg |
| Project leader | Mario Illien | Paolo Martinelli | Masao Kimura<br>Tenji Sakaj | Nick Hayes |
| Race department staff | 400 (F1 + CART) | 150 | 160 | ~ 300 |
| Engines built in 1998 | 63 | ~ 100 | + 80 | ~ 300 |
| Race engineer | Mario Illien | Giuseppe D'Agostino | Tenji Sakaj | Jim Brett |
| No of engines at races | 10 - 12 | 12 | 9 - 10 | 9 - 12 |
| Steps | - | 3 | 6 | 4 |

| SUPERTEC | PEUGEOT | PETRONAS | ARROWS | FORD |
|---|---|---|---|---|
| FB 01 | A18 Ev 4/5 | Petronas 047 03 A/B | A 20 | ZETEC - R VJM2 |
| 2996.6 cmc | 2998.3 cmc | 2998.3 cmc | 2998.1 cmc | 2998.0 cmc |
| 10 - V 71° | 10 - V 72° | 10 - V 80° | 10 - V 72° | 10 - V 72° |
| 96.00 x 41.40 | 93.00 x 44.14* | 95.00 x 42.30* | 92.00 x 45.10 | 91.00 x 46.10* |
| 13.0 : 1 | 13.2 : 1* | 13.0 : 1* | 12.5 : 1 | 12.8 : 1* |
| 4 pneumatic | 4 pneumatic | 4 pneumatic | 4 pneumatic | 4 pneumatic |
| 16.800 (Q 17.000) | 16.500 (Q 16.800)* | 16.700* (Q 17.000)* | 16.000 (Q 16.500) | 16.200 (Q 16.500) |
| 750 CV (Q 780 CV) | 760 CV* (Q 775 CV)* | 755 CV* (Q 765 CV)* | 710 CV* (Q 720 CV)* | 710 CV* (Q 720 CV*) |
| 6 | 6 | 6 | 6 | 6 |
| Moving trumpets | Fixed | Moving trumpets | Moving trumpets | Fixed |
| Electro-Hydraulic | Electro-Hydraulic | Electro-Hydraulic | Electro-Hydraulic | Butterfly with hydraulic actuator |
| Magneti Marelli | TAG - Electr. Sys 2000 | Magneti Marelli | TAG - Electr. Sys 2000 | Magneti Marelli |
| Light alloy | Light alloy | Light alloy | Aluminium alloy | Aluminium alloy |
| 623 mm | 620 mm | 618 mm | 608 mm | 605 mm |
| 545 mm | 512 mm | 538 mm | 590 mm | 520 mm |
| 390 mm | 393 mm | 478 mm | 520 mm | 450 mm |
| 122 kg | 120 kg | 122 kg | 115 kg | 123 kg* |
| Bruno Michel | Jean Pierre Boudy | Osamu Goto | Brian Hart | Mark Parish |
| 150 | 180 | - | - | 60 |
| 90 | 60 | 120 | - | 130 |
| Denis Chevrier | Guy Audoux | Osamu Gotu | John Hilton | Roger Griffiths |
| 24 - 30 | 10 - 12 | 8 | 8 | 10 |
| 2 | 4 | 2 | 2 | 2 |

**MERCEDES**
Minor step at each race.

**FERRARI**
3 steps:
48 Australia,
48 B qualifying Canada,
race G. Britain,
48C qualifying Europe,
race Malaysia.

**MUGEN HONDA**
6 steps:
A Australia, B S. Marino,
C France, D G. Britain,
E Belgium, SS qualifying
Malaysia, race Japan.

**FORD CR1 (Stewart)**
4 steps.
2 values refer to height including
or excluding airbox.

**SUPERTEC**
2 steps:
A qualifying S. Marino,
race Spain,
B qualifying Europa,
race Malesia.

**PEUGEOT**
6 steps:
EV2 Australia,
EV4 only qualifying from S. Marino,
EV4 race from G. Britain,
EV5 only qualifying from France,
EV7 only qualifying from Europe,
EV5 race Malaysia.

**PETRONAS**
2 steps:
A Australia,
B France.

**ARROWS**
2 steps:
A S. Marino,
B G. Britain.

**FORD (Minardi)**
2 steps:
VJM1 S. Marino,
VJM2 Germany.

Second line values refer
to second step

Q = Qualifying

*   Estimated value
    by Ing. E. Benzing

# Engines '99

In the technical literature 1999 will go down as the year of the historic conquest of the 800 hp threshold by the most advanced of the 3000 cc Formula 1 engines. This achievement represents a specific power output of 267 hp per litre, a record for naturally aspirated four-stroke units. What is remarkable is that given the current climate of paranoid secrecy that has developed in the sector (significantly, the unforgettable Enzo Ferrari loved to point out that he had never lost a Grand Prix through making public the technical data of one of his engines), such an important fact might have passed unnoticed were it not for independent calculations based on various performance parameters. When I pointed this out to Mario Illien, who chronologically was the first of the current crop of engineers to produce a V10 with this prodigious output, I noted a distinct air of regret, almost as if he hoped all constructors would once again provide the exhaustive technical information available in times gone by.

If we can now reliably talk of 800 hp outputs, it is thus exclusively due to the calculation of total drag that can be made preferably with the data relating to the fastest circuits or those with a straight of a certain length, at the end of which is a brief stabilising section in which the forces that oppose the advancement of the vehicle and the total forces available at the periphery of the driven wheels are balanced. It is at this point that Tag-Heuer installed their Speed Trap, to record momentary speed. With this factor known, the rolling resistance of the tyres is calculated via an equation with coefficients varying according to the track surface characteristics and the main characteristics of the tyre itself. The calculation of aerodynamic drag, a quadratic function of speed, requires a relatively simple definition (via the acquisition of CAD images) of the frontal area of the car and complex research into its nondimensional drag coefficient or Cx. This value is determined by means of a mathematical model that I have developed over decades of calculations and that permits innumerable comparisons between different bodies (and interference between them), some demonstrated in the wind tunnel, others simulated and still others such as the wing profiles, perfectly calculable. Drag due to ground-effect is approximated in an empirical-theoretical fashion according to the shape of the underbody and its established ground clearance. The final result, in the form of rounded-up average values, appears in the table where it is easy to see that only one engine supplier (Supertec) expressly declares the power output achieved while only two constructors (Supertec and Arrows) respect the traditional sporting ethic of declaring bore and stroke dimensions.

Compared with the power outputs of the 1998 engines, the 1999 figures cannot always be explained in terms of the usual increments in maximum engine speed that in some cases were slight and account for around 3 hp per 100 rpm. The most significant advances were in fact as a result of profound redesigns and the introduction of innovative materials. In two cases (Ilmor-Mercedes and Ford) these included beryllium which the FIA is to ban from 2001 after already having forbidden its use in brake calipers. Given the universal V10 engine architecture, the figures (see table) relating to the weight and length of the engines, the only data currently divulged by the manufacturers (with the exception of Ferrari), allow the most advanced units to be identified. With regards weight, 3 categories of around 120, 110 and 100 kg group the oldest engines, development versions and those using the lightest materials respectively. The same is true of engine length as it appears to be impossible to go below 600 mm without the use of ultra-thin crankcase walls and cylinder liners in beryllium, with differences of around 2.5 mm between the bore and the centre distances. Furthermore, the use of ultra-light pistons affects the resistance to greater accelerations and inertia of all the reciprocating parts. This explains the rise of the Ilmor-Mercedes V10: with the old stroke/bore ratio S/B = 0.51 (bore 91 mm for a very compact combustion chamber), the maximum engine speed of 17,000 rpm corresponded to a maximum piston acceleration of 88,600 m/s$^2$; the same figure is achieved at 17,400 rpm with the current bore of around 93 mm (S/B = 0.47). Similarly, the record of 89,700 m/s$^2$ achieved by the new Ford CR-1 would not have allowed a maximum engine speed of 17,500 rpm (the threshold was reached in 4 steps that imposed engine speed restrictions to guarantee race stability) with the previous S/B values. This can be seen in the diagram (engine speed with reference to bore diameter and the S/B ratio) in which the maximum acceleration curves indicate the progress made at the dawn of the new millennium. We have reached peaks of 25 and 40 m/s in terms of average and maximum piston speeds.

The remarkable efficiency achieved by the Ferrari 048 (3 evolutions during the year) remains exemplary, albeit without extensive use of beryllium, but was based on the lowest S/B ratio of 0.43. From the basic architecture retained in the B version, through to the C ver-

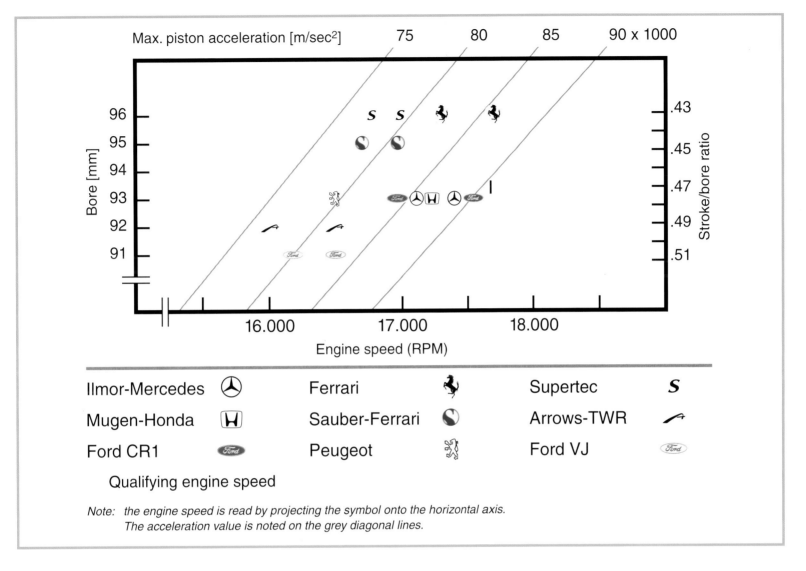

Max. piston acceleration [m/sec²]    75    80    85    90 x 1000

| Ilmor-Mercedes | ⊕ | Ferrari | 🐎 | Supertec | *S* |
| Mugen-Honda | Ⓗ | Sauber-Ferrari | ◑ | Arrows-TWR | ✍ |
| Ford CR1 | *Ford* | Peugeot | 🦁 | Ford VJ | *Ford* |

Qualifying engine speed

*Note: the engine speed is read by projecting the symbol onto the horizontal axis.*
*The acceleration value is noted on the grey diagonal lines.*

sion, it is possible (through CAD enhanced photographic documents) to identify a slight modification of the S/B ratio. In fact, the official description published on the launch of the 048/C spoke of «lowering and lightening of the crankshaft assembly», objectives achievable by means of a reduction of the stroke dimension, whilst the bore of 96 mm, in alternative according to estimates to 95 mm, had already been tried, in harmony with earlier Renault preferences that, following the withdrawal of the Régie, were conserved by the Mécachrome and Supertec engineers. The latter are to be applauded for having always declared the specifications of their engines, thus correctly enriching the technical literature. With these developments, the Ferrari 048/C engine, which was also surprising for the detail design of its cylinder block with the now generalised elimination of the oil sump (lower centre of gravity), was able to spin at 17,700 rpm without suffering the most extreme stresses. In fact, at these speeds the

maximum piston accelerations (see diagram) were only 86,100 m/s², whilst with the S/B ratio corresponding to a bore of 95 mm the figure would be 88,000 m/s², up there with the most highly stressed V10s close to the 90,000 m/s2 threshold.

In all cases, however, the tendency was towards large diameter cylinders and consequently reduced strokes, with a low connecting-rod ratio and piston pins close to the crowns. Even the Arrows engine, from the excellent Brian Hart line, passed from a bore of 91 mm to 92 mm in its second evolution. The intermediate positions of first-rate engines such as the Mugen-Honda and the Peugeot also mirrored this process during their intensive development. Formula 1 engine design thus conserved a clear division between privileging torque, with relatively long strokes, and high engine speeds with wide bores, despite the similarities in thermodynamic and mechanical efficiency. What is cer-

tain is that the lower S/B ratio of 0.43 which leaves ample room to development of the crankshaft assembly, will allow a more rapid passage to engine speeds of 18,000 rpm and beyond. The diagram clearly illustrates this fact if the symbols of the Ferrari and Supertec engines are moved parallel to the x-axis from the 80,000/85,000 m/s² area to the 90,000 m/s2 curve that, at least for the present, represents a formidable target.

*Enrico Benzing*

# The New REGULATIONS

**F**ollowing the upheaval of the previous season with the reduction in the maximum width of the cars and the abolition of slick tyres that effectively gave rise to a new formula, the FIA made only slight modifications to the technical regulations for '99. There were two main aims behind the changes: a further reduction in the performance of the cars and the continuous improvement of active safety. The first objective was pursued via the addition of a fourth groove on the front tyres, a decision which had the desired effects given that over the season slower lap times were recorded at all tracks with the exception of Interlagos. With regards safety, the impact speed of the frontal crash test was increased, a further lateral impact test was introduced in correspondence with the driver's legs to avoid the kind of injury suffered by Panis at the 1997 Canadian GP and the height of the roll bar protecting the driver's head was increased. The most conspicuous changes to the regulations in terms of safety, however, concerned two sectors; the introduction of retention cables for the wheels to prevent them detaching from the car and hitting the driver or even flying into the crowd as happened at the start of the '98 Belgian GP, and the seat extractable with the driver to facilitate rescue operations in the case of an accident and to avoid further damage to the spine.

## FRONTAL CRASH TEST
(ART. 16.2)

The impact speed of the frontal crash test to which all the cars had to be subjected before the start of the championship was increased from 12 to 13 kph. The test is carried out with a mass of 780 kg and the chassis has to have the fuel tank full of water and carry a 75 kg dummy and extinguishers. During the test the deceleration in the first 150 mm and the peak deceleration exerted on the dummy must not exceed 5g and 60g per 3 m/s respectively. The survival cell, the safety-belt mounts and the extinguisher system must emerge from the test undamaged.

## 4th TYRE GROOVE AND DIMENSIONS
(ART. 12.4.1)

A fourth groove was added to the front tyres, bringing them into line with the '98 norms for rear covers. This measure reduced the contact area by 7% with respects to the previous year, bringing the total diminution to 23% compared with the slicks of '97. A maximum front tyre width (355 mm) was adopted to restrict the escalation that began in '98 to compensate for the reduction in contact area. The minimum width for the front tyres (305 mm) remained in force, as did the maximum width at the rear (365 mm) And the maximum diameter (660 mm front and rear). In practice the only difference between the front and rear tyres in the 1999 season, both having 4 grooves, was 10 mm extra width.

'98

'99

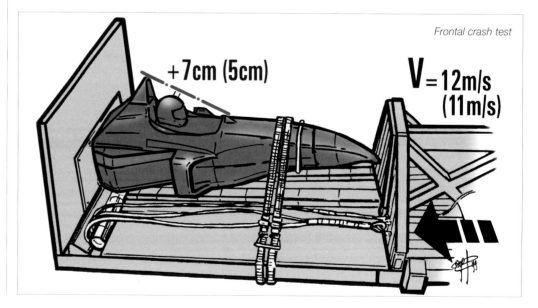

+7cm (5cm)

$V = 12$m/s (11m/s)

*Frontal crash test*

*Wheel retention*

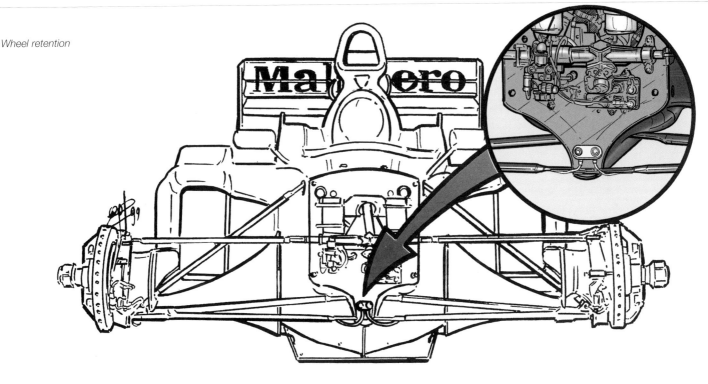

## ROLL STRUCTURE
(ART. 15.2.2)
The minimum distance between the drivers' helmet and the line linking the two roll structures was increased from 5 to 7 cm to guarantee greater protection for the drivers in the case of overturning or accidents such as the one that occurred at the start of the '98 Canadian GP.

## LATERAL CRASH TEST
(ART.18.2)
A third lateral crash test in the pedal-box area (along with those to the sides of the fuel tank and in the area of the cockpit centre) was introduced to avoid injuries of the kind suffered by Panis in '97. A force of 25,000 kN must be applied for 30 seconds. Each chassis must pass a total of 12 crash tests and inspections before the start of the season. The data collected during these tests carried out in the presence of a FIA technical delegate are stored in three transponders buried in the survival cells at the three points shown in orange in the drawing. At the GPs the scrutineers use a device produced by the German firm Trovan to check the data regarding the tests passed by that survival cell.

## WHEEL RETENTION
(ART. 14.7)
All cars were required to be fitted with a wheel retention system comprising a cable at least 7 mm in diameter to avoid that the wheels can detach, hitting the driver or flying into the crowd. Generally these cables passed between the suspension arms and were fixed to the chassis as shown in the drawing. This norm attracted criticism because in certain cases, the wheel trapped against the chassis during the impact sawed into the survival cell, as happened with Zonta's BAR in Brazil and Schumacher's Ferrari at Silverstone.

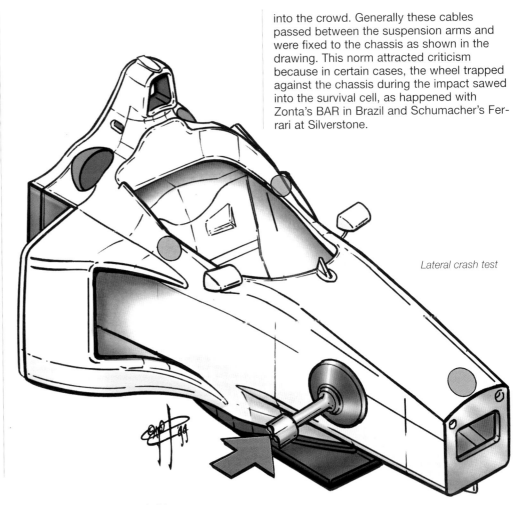

*Lateral crash test*

## EXTRACTABLE SEAT
### (ART.14.8)
In order to facilitate rescue operations in the event of a crash an extractable seat jointly developed by the American firm Lear, Stewart and the FIA medical delegate was introduced. The seat must be equipped with a system of belts and a neck brace to reduce to the minimum the consequences of possible spinal injuries. The drawing shows the transverse belts and the mounts for the other 4 necessary to extract the seat from the cockpit.

## WING VERIFICATION
### (ART.3.15)
At the second race of the season, following disputes ongoing since winter testing, the FIA introduced a new check to verify the true degree of flexibility of the rear wings. As seen in the drawing, this involves a structure attached to the rear wing and subjecting it to traction by means of a screw. A load of 100 kg is applied, measured with a dynamometer attached to the structure.

# Controversy in '99

The 1999 season will long be remembered for the serious accident involving Michael Schumacher and his Ferrari early in the British GP. This episode conditioned the rest of the season and not only in terms of the final championship standings. Criticism was directed at the rubber safety structures and the wheel retention system that in effect cut into the front part of the F399's safety cell. Arguments over the interpretation of the technical regulations instead began even before the start of the opening race of the '99 season, in line with what has become something of a tradition for the Formula 1 circus. What came under fire this time round was the use of flexible rear wings in pre-season testing (in late '97 it had been the turn of the front wings to be taken to extremes), even though the regulations have prohibited any form of variation in the incidence of the aerodynamic surfaces since as long ago as 1969. Pre-season testing was in fact punctuated by a series of dramatic and dangerous rear wing failures due both to the spasmodic recourse to lighter cars and the greater vibrations provoked by the latest generation of 10-cylinder engines. One of the major features of the '99 cars was, in fact, that they were significantly underweight, the leading teams managing to pare up to 50 kg off the minimum weight limit. The repeated wing failures, combined with the arguments over their degree of flexibility, allowed the FIA to use safety as a pretext for the immediate introduction of a further check regarding the flexibility of the wings (see page 22) during the Thursday scrutineering from the second race in Brazil.

Discontent was aroused by Jordan's borderline interpretation of the regulations regarding the protection either side of the driver's head, although no official protests were lodged. Once again the FIA was obliged to adjust its sights, modifying the regulations in view of the start of the first season of the new millennium. Suspicions continued to be aroused regarding irregularities in the cars' various electronic management systems that had been further restricted at the end of the '98 season. As usual, attention was focused on the possible uses of traction, braking and differential control and assisted starting systems. Considerable suspicion surrounded the retirements of both Jordans, Hill at the first corner after the start and Frentzen at the same corner but after a pit stop, at the GP of Europe. The most remarkable incident was, however, the immediate disqualification of the two Ferraris after their stunning 1-2 success at Sepang in the Malaysian GP. The disqualification came as a result of a minimal irregularity in the vertical projection of the new barge boards introduced at the preceding GP of Europe. The verdict delivered at the Paris appeal court restored victory to Maranello, confirming the absurdity of disqualification for an infraction that, in any case, had no influence on performance. At the same time, however, the episode did arouse suspicions that the leading teams were using flexible rear diffusers.

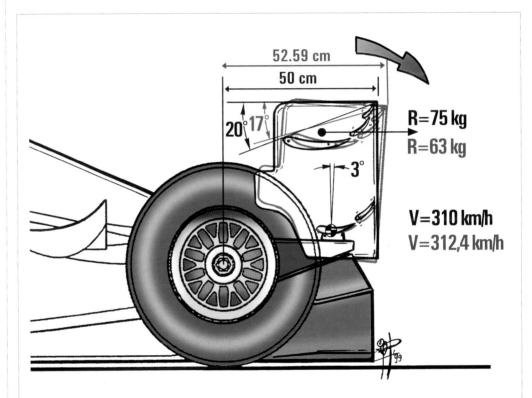

## MOBILE WINGS
Thanks to the use of special supports in composite materials having a known degree of flexibility, many teams got round the regulations stating that every aerodynamic device should be rigidly attached to the central suspended part of the car. As highlighted in the drawing, the advantages of such loopholes are considerable: a rear wing assembly that flexes backwards by just 3° is sufficient to obtain an increase in maximum speed in the order of 2.4 kph, with a reduction in drag of no less than 8 kg. While on the one hand it is difficult to quantify the degree of tolerance associated with the term «rigidly attached», it is very easy to outlaw a wing that flexes backwards, measuring the degree to which it exceeds the maximum permitted rear overhang of 50 cm. The technical regulation is very precise and states that a car must conform to the norms throughout a race meeting. A flexure of just 3°, in fact, ensures that the maximum overhang is exceeded by no less than 2.59 cm, a clear-cut breach of the rules.

## JORDAN

The reduction of the area either side of the driver's head on the Jordans was very controversial. The regulations regarding the protection structures came into force in '96 and was immediately the root of arguments when Williams (below) introduced small tabs either side in order to reduce the height of the protection structures, theoretically fixed by the parameters highlighted in the drawing below. From the next season most of the teams followed Newey's lead, but Jordan 199 is certainly the extreme example. In practice the chassis is flat (1) in the area either side of the cockpit and the protection structures are reduced to the vertical fins (2) alone. For the 2000 season the FIA has imposed the use of a control template.

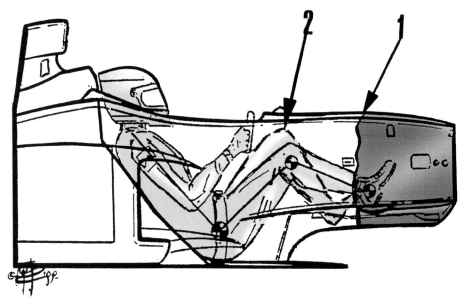

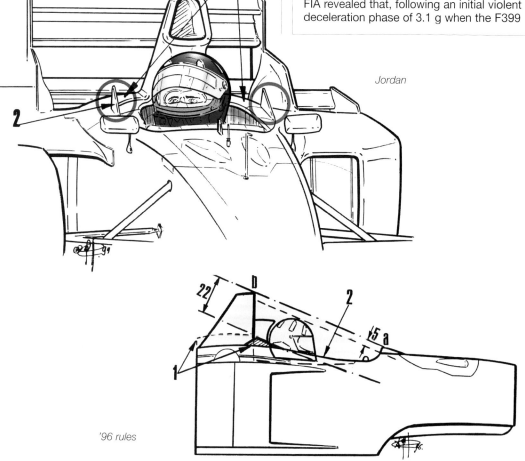

Jordan

'96 rules

## SCHUMACHER'S ACCIDENT

Michael Schumacher's dramatic crash at Stowe on the first lap of the British GP was caused by a leak from the bleed nipple of the left rear brake (see the brakes chapters, page 39). The telemetric data supplied by the FIA revealed that, following an initial violent deceleration phase of 3.1 g when the F399 was travelling at 306 kph, this value dropped to just 2.1 g due to the blockage of the rear wheels at 204 kph. The impact with the tyre wall occurred at 107 kph after the car had ploughed through the sand trap with the front wheels locked with deceleration dropping to 1.1 g. The injuries suffered by the German driver concentrated on his right leg

## THE MALAYSIAN GP

The post-race atmosphere at the first Malaysian GP was red-hot with both Ferraris disqualified for an irregularity discovered by the authorities consisting of a missing 10 mm in the vertical projection of the new bargeboards behind the front wheels, introduced at the preceding GP of Europe. The regulation concerning the horizontal shadow plate determined by the vertical projection of every bodywork element in the area within the tangents of the wheels of both axles was introduced along with the obligatory flat bottom in 1983 (art 3.12.1) in order to close possible loopholes. In the past even rear-view mirrors were affected by what is in effect a bureaucratic norm with no technical significance. The missing section did not, in reality, have any effect on the performance of the car, in contrast with the case at the '96 French GP when during practice Irvine's Ferrari was found to have barge-boards that were 15 mm too high in an area that clearly influenced aerodynamics (he was relegated to the last row of the grid). Ferrari's appeal in Paris restored championship points to both the drivers and the manufacturer, partly because imprecision in the system of measurement employed at Sepang was revealed. The infraction was, in fact, restricted to a matter of just 5 mm, and came within the accepted tolerance for the components. There

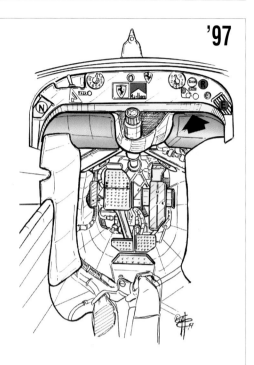

'97

vival cells, allowing them to bend their legs (2), and the removal of all suspension elements from the pedalbox area, checked by the scrutineers by inserting a wooden block into the chassis (see drawing). A comparison between the cockpit of the F399 and that of the '97 Ferrari, right, shows how the rib at the

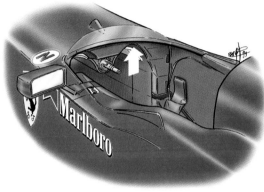

were caused by the failure of the chassis in the area indicated by the arrow (1) (damage aggravated by the right wheel which in part sawed into the survival cell), but were restricted thanks to the new safety norms introduced by the FIA in the '98 season. There were two particularly important factors: the greater space available to the drivers within the sur-

level of the instruments was lower, but above all lacked the two niches (indicated by the arrow) that allow extra room for the legs, a feature very useful at the moment of impact and during subsequent rescue operations.

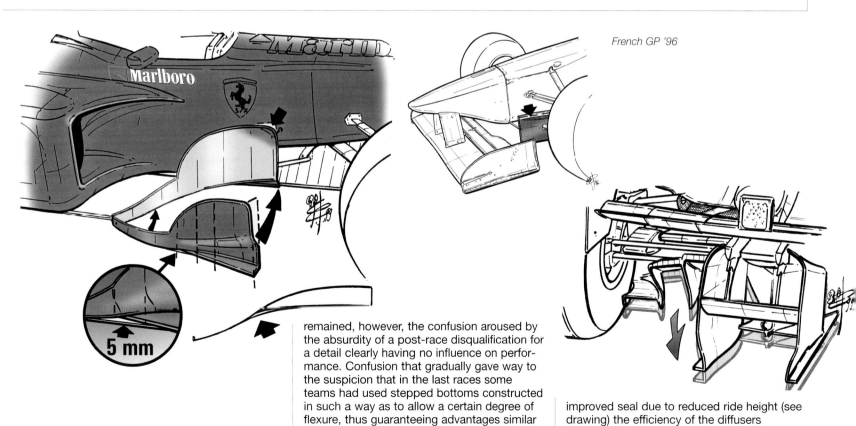

*French GP '96*

5 mm

remained, however, the confusion aroused by the absurdity of a post-race disqualification for a detail clearly having no influence on performance. Confusion that gradually gave way to the suspicion that in the last races some teams had used stepped bottoms constructed in such a way as to allow a certain degree of flexure, thus guaranteeing advantages similar to those provided by the flexible wings contested at the start of the season. With an

improved seal due to reduced ride height (see drawing) the efficiency of the diffusers increased, thus providing greater downforce and rear-end stability.

# New Features and
# TRENDS

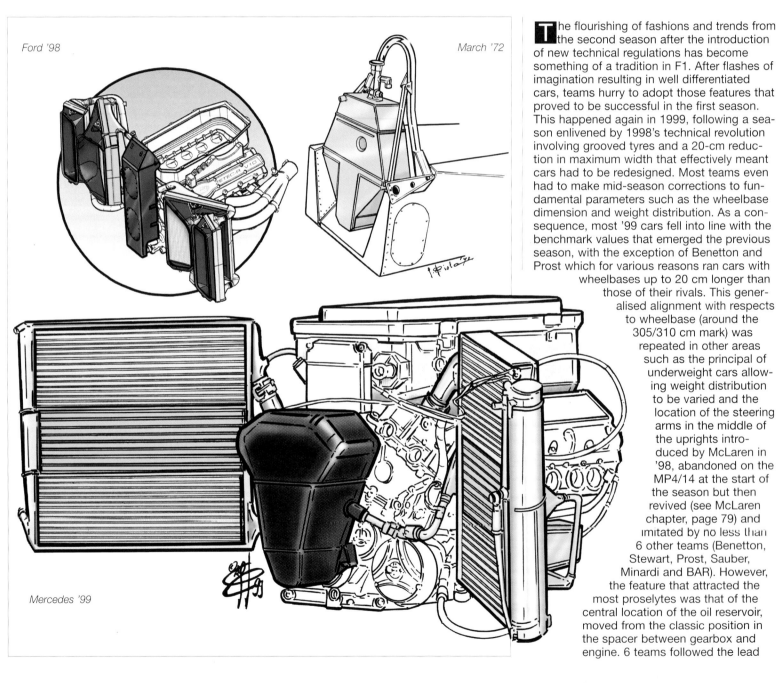

Ford '98

March '72

Mercedes '99

The flourishing of fashions and trends from the second season after the introduction of new technical regulations has become something of a tradition in F1. After flashes of imagination resulting in well differentiated cars, teams hurry to adopt those features that proved to be successful in the first season. This happened again in 1999, following a season enlivened by 1998's technical revolution involving grooved tyres and a 20-cm reduction in maximum width that effectively meant cars had to be redesigned. Most teams even had to make mid-season corrections to fundamental parameters such as the wheelbase dimension and weight distribution. As a consequence, most '99 cars fell into line with the benchmark values that emerged the previous season, with the exception of Benetton and Prost which for various reasons ran cars with wheelbases up to 20 cm longer than those of their rivals. This generalised alignment with respects to wheelbase (around the 305/310 cm mark) was repeated in other areas such as the principal of underweight cars allowing weight distribution to be varied and the location of the steering arms in the middle of the uprights introduced by McLaren in '98, abandoned on the MP4/14 at the start of the season but then revived (see McLaren chapter, page 79) and imitated by no less than 6 other teams (Benetton, Stewart, Prost, Sauber, Minardi and BAR). However, the feature that attracted the most proselytes was that of the central location of the oil reservoir, moved from the classic position in the spacer between gearbox and engine. 6 teams followed the lead

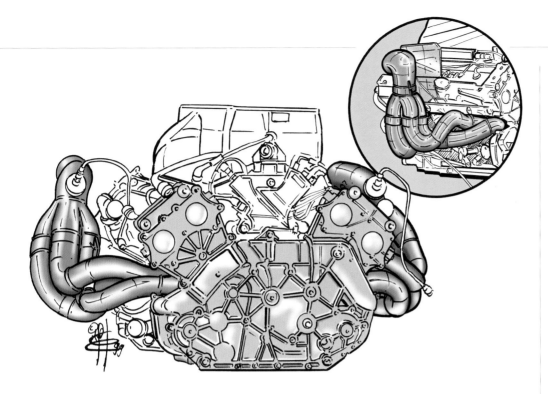

## HIGH EXHAUSTS

Another feature destined to proliferate is that of the high exhausts introduced by Ferrari at the '98 Spanish GP and adopted on the F399 from the outset. This arrangement allows the working temperature to be reduced throughout the critical lower engine and gearbox area, with advantages that compensate for the negative effects of the flow of hot air blowing through the equally critical area of the upper part of the engine cover in front of the rear wing. It was already being imitated in the '99 season by 2 other teams, Stewart and Prost. The first at the Austrian GP, the second at the Belgian GP. Comparative tests were also performed during the season by McLaren, Williams and Benetton. The two drawings represent the variants adopted by Ferrari on the '98 F300 (in the circle) and carried over to the F399.

established in '98 by Alan Jenkins with the Stewart and John Barnard with the Arrows (McLaren, Jordan, Benetton, Prost, Minardi and BAR), which meant that 8 out of the eleven teams disputing the championship had adopted the feature. What is most interesting about this technical revolution which provided significant advantages such as a greater concentration of weight close to the centre of gravity, a reduction in the mass of the various pipes and cleaner aerodynamics around the critical zone between the rear wheels, is that it was nothing more than a return to the past, as testified by the oil reservoir on the March 721 (drawing, top) from 1972. It was McLaren with the M23 of '76 which first relocated the oil reservoir within the gearbox spacer, a position that became universal but is now destined to disappear before the start of the first race of the new millennium. As can be seen, the trapezoidal McLaren oil reservoir is very similar to that of the old March, while that of the Stewart '98 is tall and narrow.

## FORD CR-1

The object of the most fruitless spying in the '99 season was the new Ford CR-1 engine, its compact dimensions making it always easy to conceal from prying eyes even on the start-line. This was the lightest engine (99 kg) of the entire batch of ten-cylinder units raced, partly thanks to the use of sophisticated materials such as beryllium and carbonfibre. The drawing shows how the pumps (oil in the centre) and ancillary organs are external. The design and ribbing of the cover (presumably in magnesium alloy) is indicative of the position of the gear-train and it can be deduced that Ford has abandoned its traditional integrated system which also comprised a lower chain. The camshaft drive at the front of the engine is composed of a train of small gears driving the right-hand camshaft only, the left-hand shaft of the pair being driven directly off the first, with less overall friction losses attributable to the system. The valve angle must be relatively narrow.

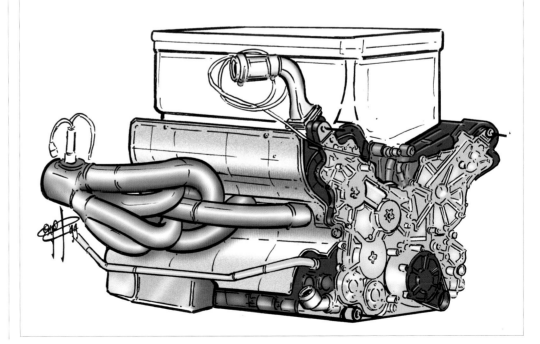

## PROST

Prost introduced two brand-new features, although only the first, a new master cylinder location, was actually employed. The use of two pads identical in diameter to the brake discs instead never got beyond the testing stage.

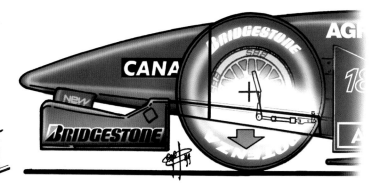

## MASTER CYLINDERS

The first feature was conceived by that fount of F1 wisdom, John Barnard, the designer who with the introduction of the semi-automatic gearbox on the Ferrari 640 of '89 revolutionised modern Formula 1. Freed of responsibility for the entire project, his great attention to detail focused on selected areas of the car. In '94 he had already introduced a new master cylinder layout on the Ferrari 412 T1, since universally adopted. Last year he developed a new brake caliper with AP, at first exclusively for Arrows and subsequently supplied to the other teams. For the Prost the English wizard dreamed up a new easily accessible external location for the master cylinders in the lower part of the chassis, making the pedalbox area less crowded and safer. The unusual view from below shows the large brake pedal (1) and the two linking pistons for the pumps (2) with the right-hand one reserved for the rear circuit and fitted with an additional spring (the brakes chapter). The very sophisticated electronically controlled hydraulic rocker (3) manages bias between the two axles. The electro valves (4) are located within the chassis.

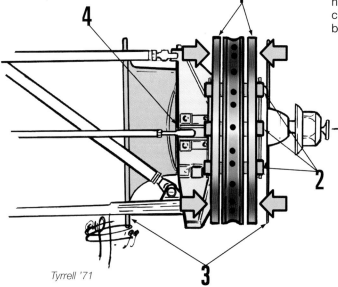

*Tyrrell '71*

## PADS/DISCS

The braking system composed of two large pads the same diameter (278 mm) as the brake discs (1) inspired by the systems used on aircraft was never raced. The system did not involve the twin discs previously used on the Tyrell OO1 of '71 and then tried again on the '85 Williams FW10. The simplified diagram shows the 6 pistons (2) fixed to two star-shaped flanges mounted on the usual fabricated hub carriers (4) and the shields (3) fitted both inside and out to avoid indiscreet photographs during testing. This feature was very difficult to fine-tune and could fall foul of the regulations because among the severe restrictions imposed by the FIA is one specifying a single disc per wheel, even though in this case the external pair actually act as pads.

## BENETTON FTT SYSTEM

The new Nick Wirth-designed feature involving front brakes fitted with a form of differential (1) so as to provide optimum braking force management conditioned the entire B199 project. The car had a disproportionately long wheelbase (328 cm) to compensate for the extra weight bearing on the front axle (11 kg, of which 9 accounted for by the braking system and 2 by the chassis). Wurz, especially, given that he is heavier than Fisichella, was penalised by the impossibility of adjusting weight distribution with ballast.

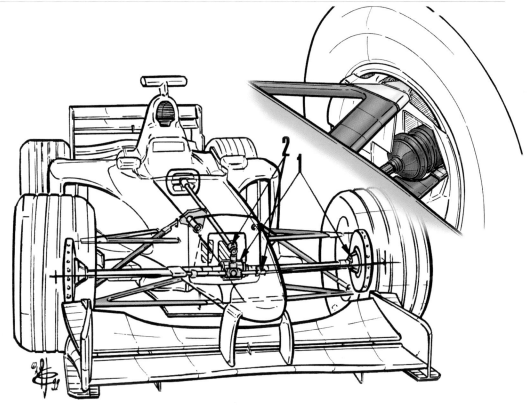

## REAR TYRE SEAL

During tyre changes, a small bodywork section was retracted and secured with a nut to avoid dangerous cuts to the tyres. When the car was ready to restart a mechanic removed the lock securing the knife-edge, thus restoring the perfect seal against the rear tyre, improving aerodynamic efficiency.

## SCHUMACHER'S HELMET

One new feature concerned not a car but rather Schumacher's helmet and was destined for further development. The secret was revealed at the Brazilian GP while the system's debut race was the San Marino GP. In practice the helmet was fitted with LED indicators in the area below the nose, repeating those mounted at the top of the steering wheel (indicated by the blue arrows). The camera car TV images frequently showed the LEDs flickering in rapid sequence as they informed the driver when to change gear. In certain light conditions the LEDs were difficult to see and so they were mounted in a shaded part of the bottom of the helmet.

# COCKPITS, PEDALS AND
## STEERING WHEELS

A After having launched steering wheel electronics in '96 Ferrari once again introduced a number of innovations in this area. At the San Marino GP Michael Schumacher used a helmet with LEDs incorporated in the lower section indicating the correct engine speed at which to change gear. At the following Monaco GP the «Rosse» featured another new and even more sophisticated steering wheel designed to facilitate the replacement of the electronic componentry without removing the wheel itself from the car. In the '99 season only 3 teams had yet to adopt the trend launched by Ferrari: Williams, Sauber and the debutante BAR; all the others featured steering wheels strongly influenced by the one introduced by Barnard on the F310 of '96. McLaren and Jordan represent separate cases, having adapted fighter aircraft-like joysticks to the driver's need to handle diverse functions with controls located directly on the wheel. McLaren also provided its drivers with individual designs that were very different, especially in the lower section. It should be noted that the major teams produced over 20 wheels for each driver. At Jean Alesi's precise request Sauber was the only team this season not to have a steering wheel-mounted clutch paddle as he does not like controlling the clutch with his hands and prefers three pedals so as to brake in the classic manner with the right foot. Among the rest of the field with two pedals, there were still some drivers who prefer right-foot braking and thus have two classically positioned, close-set pedals, as in the case of Barrichello and Herbert. Unfortunately the strenuous efforts made by the teams in the '98 season to prevent observation of the interiors of their cars continued and have restricted the descriptions of this sector which in previous seasons were more detailed.

## STEERING WHEELS TABLE
Ferrari introduced the third generation of computerised steering wheels at the Monaco GP (see the comparison with the wheel used in recent seasons on the left). The symmetri-

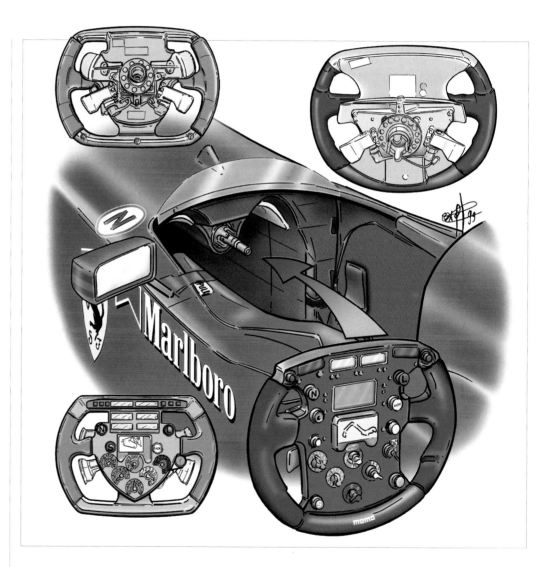

cal shape was abandoned with the new wheel being squared-off apart from a rounded lower section that allowed a more rational arrangement of the various and more numerous controls. The shape of the display was also changed with a very large central element on which the driver could choose the functions

to be visualised. The most important change was the possibility of replacing the central section, in effect all the electronic components, without taking the wheel out of the car. The circular rim was made of a self-moulding material that allowed the grip area to be personalised by the heat of the driver's hands.

## FERRARI STEERING WHEEL

The steering wheel of the F399 was even closer to a true computer. This third generation component had an even greater number of functions than the one used up to the San Marino GP. There were no less than 21 buttons, knobs and paddles available to the driver. 1) The operation of the twin gearbox paddles was unchanged, the right-hand lever being used to change up and the left-hand one to change down. 2) Button to activate the speed limiter in the pits. 3) Rear axle brake adjustment. 4) Two displays to visualise real time and lap time. 5) Tell-tales that light in rapid sequence to indicate the correct engine speed for gear changes. 6) Front axle brake bias. 7) Neutral button. 8) Main display providing basic information selected by the driver such as the gear selected, engine speed and oil and water temperatures. 9) Electrical cut-off to stop the engine. 10) Multifunction button allowing the driver to drink. 11) Knob allowing the various brake bias programmes to be selected. 12) Manual safety control for the fuel filler, generally activated automatically with the engagement of the speed limiter in the pit lane. 13) Fuel/air mixture adjustment. 14) Reset knob allowing the basic functions of the car's various control systems to be restored. 15) Electronically controlled power steering adjustment. 16) Engine mapping, strictly governed by the regulations. 17) Main display information selector. 18) Management of the various electronic throttle programmes. 19) Dual electronic clutch paddles. 20) Multifunction button to change the steering wheel display modes.

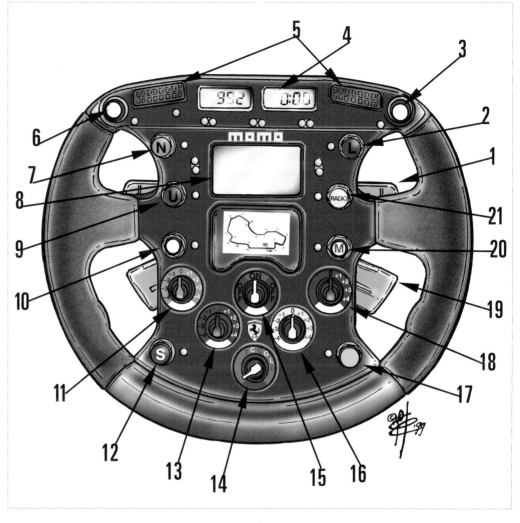

## SCHUMACHER'S PEDALS

In the '99 season Schumacher again used the two pedals with ample lateral stops that effectively lock the feet into place. The shape of the pedals and the positioning of the stops was changed slightly with respects to the first version introduced in '97, above all with regards to the lower-set squared-off brake pedal. Moreover, the upper stop is missing, replaced by a small bulkhead on the left not fitted to the '97 pedal.

## WILLIAMS

Many teams retained some form of stop either side of the pedals, similar to those introduced by Schumacher in '97. Williams, and Villeneuve in the BAR, had stops either side of the throttle (1) and brake (2) pedals and in the ankle area (3).

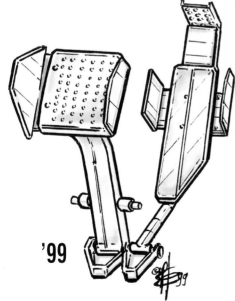

'99

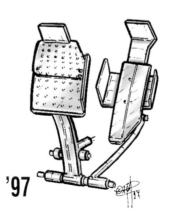

'97

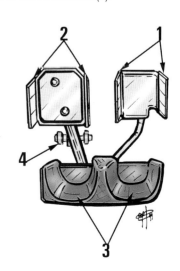

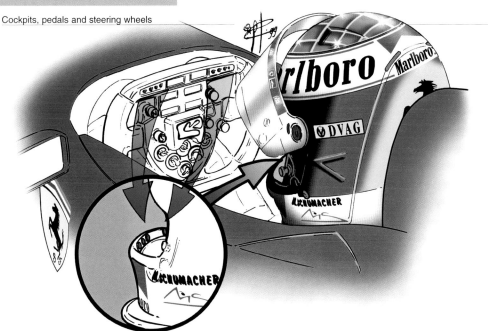

## SCHUMACHER'S HELMET

During qualifying for the San Marino GP Ferrari and Schumacher experimented with a helmet on the lower section of which had been fitted the LEDs indicating the correct engine speed at which to change gear originally mounted on the steering wheel. This location could be difficult for the driver to read in certain conditions of light. In the drawing the blue arrows show the two different positions. It should be noted that this experiment was not followed up during the rest of the season.

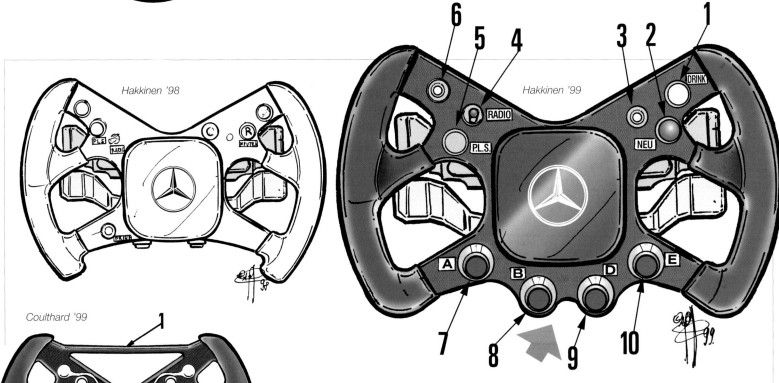

*Hakkinen '98*

*Coulthard '99*

*Hakkinen '99*

## McLAREN STEERING WHEEL

### HAKKINEN

The McLaren steering wheels were virtually unchanged and were among the few not fitted with a display visualising various data. The two drivers retained differentiated wheels, with Hakkinen keeping faith with his horizontal X-shape. A series of 4 mutifunction knobs was added at the bottom. 1) Button allowing the driver to drink. 2) Neutral. 3) Neutral selected tell-tale. 4) Radio and tell-tale (6). 5) Pit lane speed limiter. 7-8-10) Knobs controlling the various electronic throttle and clutch programmes. 9) Air-fuel mixture.

### COULTHARD

David Coulthard retained the steering wheel with a horizontal bar (1) at the top that acted as a straight ahead reference. 2) The two conspicuous extensions for the handling of the clutch in the case of a spin were also unchanged. 3) The perfectly circular lower rim was also unaltered.

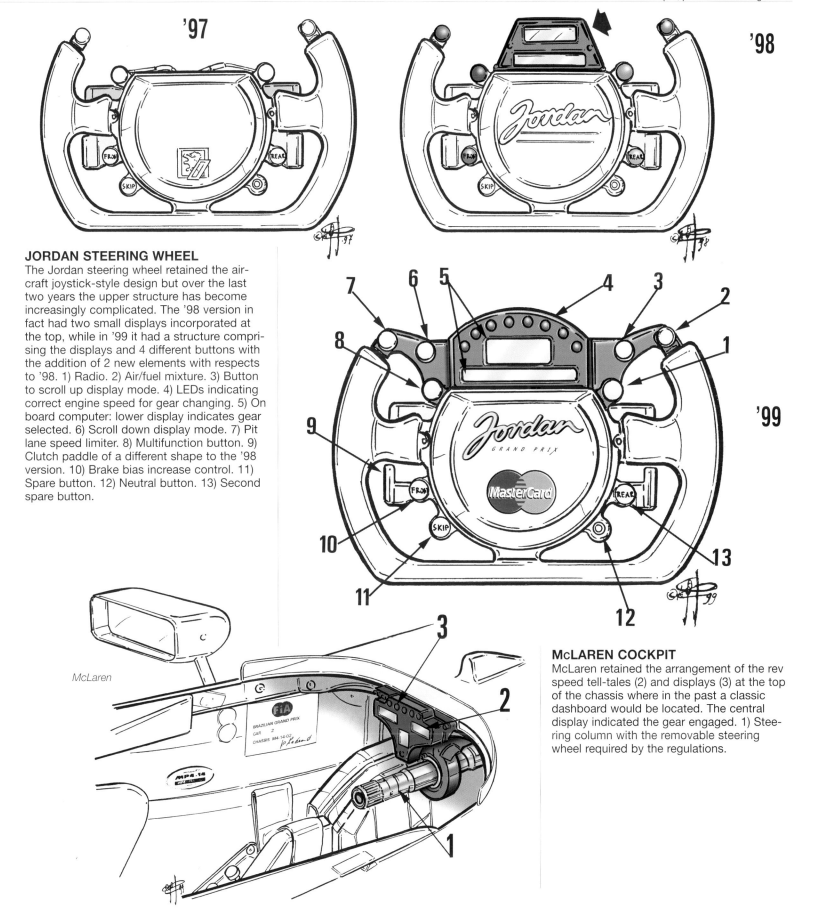

**'97**

**'98**

**'99**

## JORDAN STEERING WHEEL

The Jordan steering wheel retained the aircraft joystick-style design but over the last two years the upper structure has become increasingly complicated. The '98 version in fact had two small displays incorporated at the top, while in '99 it had a structure comprising the displays and 4 different buttons with the addition of 2 new elements with respects to '98. 1) Radio. 2) Air/fuel mixture. 3) Button to scroll up display mode. 4) LEDs indicating correct engine speed for gear changing. 5) On board computer: lower display indicates gear selected. 6) Scroll down display mode. 7) Pit lane speed limiter. 8) Multifunction button. 9) Clutch paddle of a different shape to the '98 version. 10) Brake bias increase control. 11) Spare button. 12) Neutral button. 13) Second spare button.

*McLaren*

## McLAREN COCKPIT

McLaren retained the arrangement of the rev speed tell-tales (2) and displays (3) at the top of the chassis where in the past a classic dashboard would be located. The central display indicated the gear engaged. 1) Steering column with the removable steering wheel required by the regulations.

## BENETTON STEERING WHEEL

The Benetton steering wheel was unchanged with respects to that of '98. 1) Gear change paddles. 2) Three buttons of which the one on the right energies the pit land speed limiter and the one in the centre neutral. 3) Spare button. 4-6) Scrolling up or down the display modes. 5) Engine speed and state of health tell-tales. 7) Telemetry data download port. 8) Radio. 9) Two engine mapping options selected in the pits with the car stationary. 10) Knob for the various electronic control systems, braking, throttle, clutch and so on. 11) Fuel-air mixture.

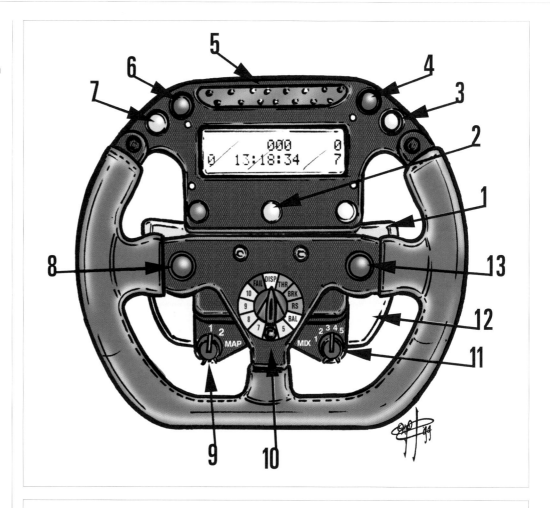

## MINARDI COCKPIT

The pedalbox area of the Minardi was very tidy and allowed the layout of the front suspension located entirely in the area in front of the pedals to be observed. This arrangement was in part dictated by the regulations introduced by FIA whereby during scrutineering a 35 cm cube must pass within the survival cell which must be free of suspension elements. 1) Protected extinguisher control. 2-3) Multifunction knobs not used during the '99 season. 4) Engine mapping, fuel-air mixture. 5) Suspension rocker. 6) Third horizontal damper. 7) Articulated anti-roll bar similar to that used by Ferrari. 8) Third damper mount on the suspension rocker. 9) Button allowing the driver to drink. 10) Neutral. 11) Rear light with tell-tale. 12) Electrical cut-off. 13) Engine start. 14) Dampers attached to the rocker and fixed to the chassis at the bottom. 15) The two large pedals have lateral stops (in yellow), the brake pedal being connected to the two master cylinders on which the electronic brake bias control acts. 16) Extinguisher.

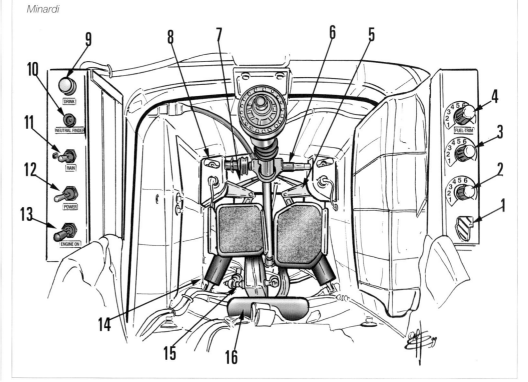

*Minardi*

## MINARDI STEERING WHEEL

The all-carbonfibre steering wheel used by Minardi was very elegant. 1) Pit lane speed limiter. 2) Brake balance towards front axle. 3-5) LEDs signalling rev speed for gear changes. 4) Display. 6) Tell-tales indicating the colour of the flags waved by the marshals. 7) Brake balance towards rear axle. 8) Radio. 9) Emergency clutch. 10) Reverse. 11) Dual clutch paddles with extensions to facilitate operation in the case of a spin. 12) Neutral. 13) Button to change the display mode.

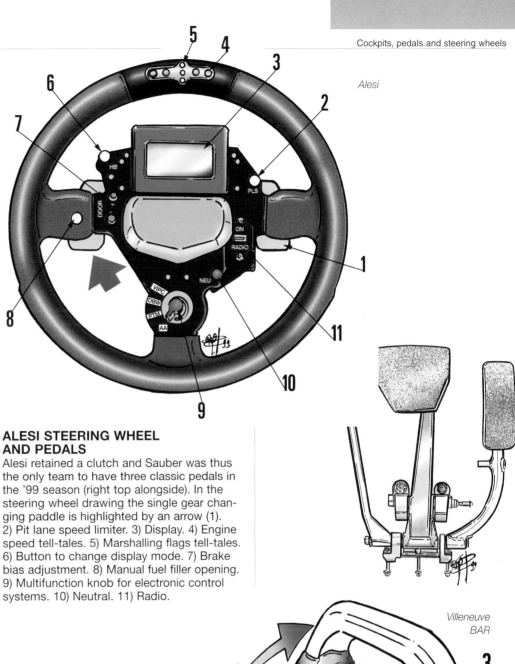

*Alesi*

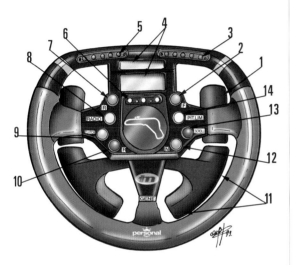

## ALESI STEERING WHEEL AND PEDALS

Alesi retained a clutch and Sauber was thus the only team to have three classic pedals in the '99 season (right top alongside). In the steering wheel drawing the single gear changing paddle is highlighted by an arrow (1). 2) Pit lane speed limiter. 3) Display. 4) Engine speed tell-tales. 5) Marshalling flags tell-tales. 6) Button to change display mode. 7) Brake bias adjustment. 8) Manual fuel filler opening. 9) Multifunction knob for electronic control systems. 10) Neutral. 11) Radio.

## VILLENEUVE STEERING WHEEL

Jacques Villeneuve remained the only driver to change both up and down gears with the right-hand paddle alone (1), a system he had used at Williams (steering wheel right) with a push-pull action (indicated by the double arrow. 2) The large clutch paddle instead remained on the right. 3) His habit of wrapping the grip area of the rim with tape was also unchanged.

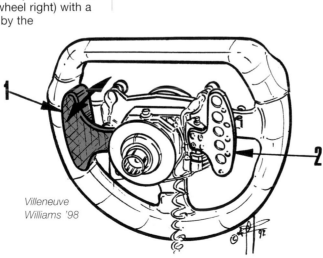

*Villeneuve Williams '98*

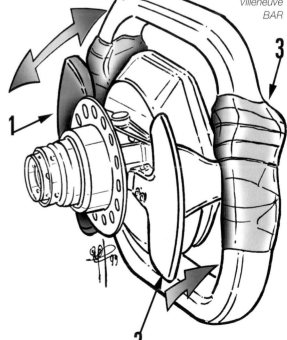

*Villeneuve BAR*

# Talking about
# BRAKES AND TYRES

The severe restrictions on braking systems introduced in '98 were retained for the '99 season. This meant that exotic materials like beryllium or metalmatrix were outlawed and calipers could be equipped with a maximum of 6 pistons with a single caliper per disc. Maximum disc thickness was just 28 mm. Specific restrictions were added regarding electronic brake bias control with no adjustments being permitted during actual braking. There was also the addition of a 4th groove to the front tyres and the consequent adoption of harder compounds which reduced the cars' grip when cornering and had a negative effect on braking performance. Well balanced braking between the front and rear axles became even more important. Much work was done on disc and pad materials and on ventilating the systems. Designers had to revise the aerodynamic compromise to obtain adequate heat disposal without excessive disturbance of the air flow in the critical area of the wheels which were 20 cm closer to the car than in '97. With the abolition of electronic brake bias control, in order to verify fall-off in performance and to ensure adequate cooling considerable fine-tuning was required to get close to the cars' grip limits, varying brake bias according to the nature of the individual circuits and 2/3 types of braking. The development work carried out on the braking system as a whole (calipers, friction materials, brake bias adjustment and cooling systems) aimed at reducing to a minimum the friction range between the onset of braking and maximum efficiency so as to obtain a more direct correlation between pedal force and braking power. In practice, the teams tried to use the various components available to personalise the braking systems according to the various cars and the drivers' driving styles.

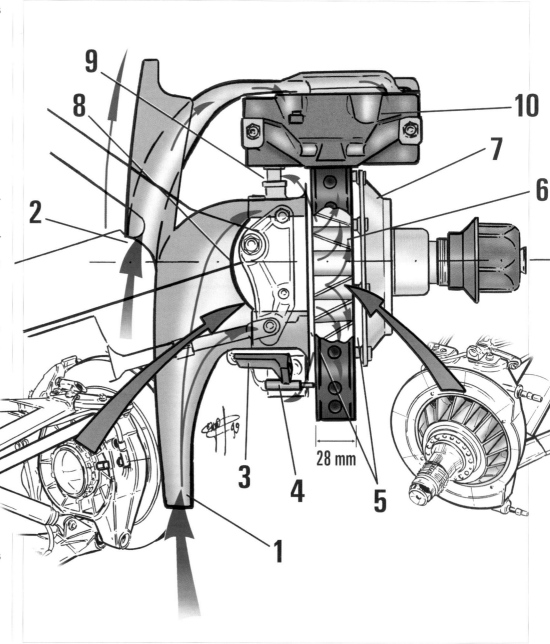

28 mm

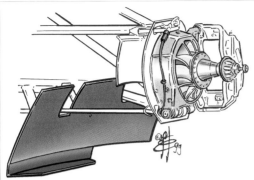

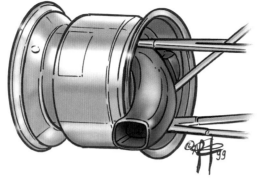

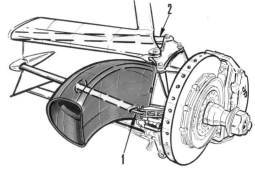

## WILLIAMS

Williams introduced conspicuously twisted fins in the central part of the upright (fabricated titanium) in place of straight ones, as shown here, to increase turbulence in the central zone and therefore brake cooling. Note the flat circular fairing of the air intake, almost completely flush with the wheel.

## FERRARI

Ferrari caused a surprise at the Canadian GP due to the unusual shape of the front brake air intakes. They drew in air from the lower part of the wing which was not ideal from an aerodynamic point of view, but provided very efficient cooling. This feature was only used on Montreal's semi-street circuit, very hard on brakes.

## McLAREN

At circuits hard on brakes McLaren used these large, very rounded intakes capable of drawing in large quantities of air. The Hitco discs required relatively low working temperatures compared with the C.I. discs. After the Austrian GP the steering arm, previously faired into the upper wishbone (2) passed through the middle of the intake (1).

## BRAKE AIR INTAKE

This drawing provides a diagrammatic view of the brake cooling system.

1) The principal intake that channels air towards the central part of the hub.
2) Secondary intake for cooling the caliper (10). Note also the fairing of the intake itself to improve the efficiency of the flow towards the body of the car.
3) Disc temperature sensor.
4) Disc thickness sensor.
5) Space between the coupling flange and the disc.
6) Fins within the upright to increase brake disc cooling, highlighted in the detail, right, depicting an upright with the disc removed.
7) Disc mounting flange.
8) Sphere attached to the central zone to accelerate the air flow in the two lateral channels indicated by the arrows visible in the drawing, left.
9) Attachment of the caliper to the disc. Regulations permit only two mounting points.
10) Caliper with maximum of 6 pistons.

Much work was carried out. in the '99 season to improve and render more constant brake cooling, as can be seen in the drawings on the facing page.

## CAST-IRON DISCS

Surprisingly, at the Austrian GP Williams reintroduced cast-iron brake discs to F1 for the first time since '85 (although the same team had tested them in '97 too), using them in qualifying only for the following races. This feature, which on paper makes little sense as it increases unsprung weight while uprights in titanium and other sophisticated solutions try to reduce it, responded to Zanardi's request and to increase the working temperature of the

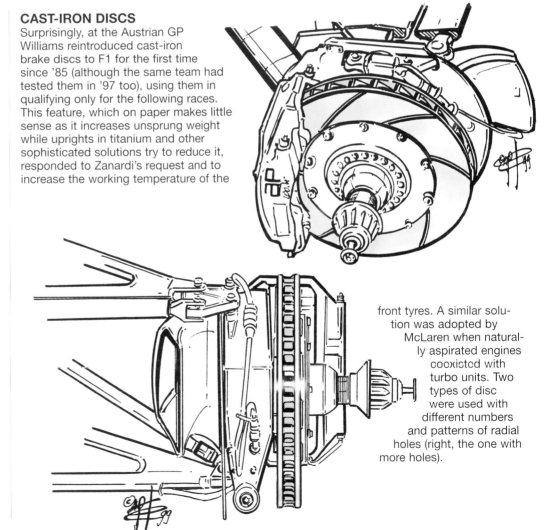

front tyres. A similar solution was adopted by McLaren when naturally aspirated engines coexisted with turbo units. Two types of disc were used with different numbers and patterns of radial holes (right, the one with more holes).

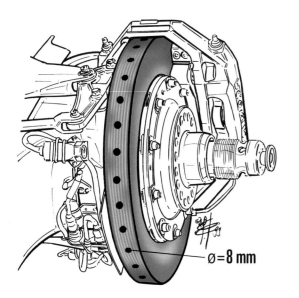

⌀=8 mm

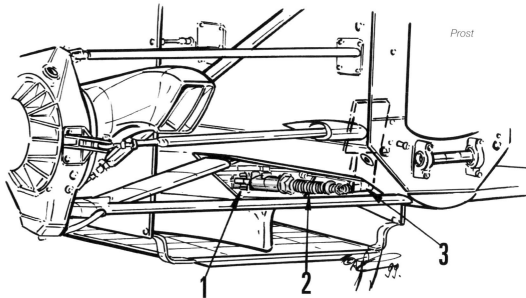

*Prost*

1
2
3

## NEW FEATURES

At the Belgian GP Brembo introduced CCR discs made by the American firm Als on Salo's Ferrari. Of aeronautical provenance, they were made from a new material distinguishable from the Carbon Industrie components by the presence of light streaks. The radial holes were arranged as on the French discs (2 close together and 1 further apart) but were 8 mm in diameter against 10 mm. CCR is a very stable, less critical material at the operating temperatures of C.I.'s P7 introduced in '98 exclusively on the Ferraris and subsequently supplied to the other teams in '99. Both Schumacher and Irvine used these discs at the Malaysian GP.

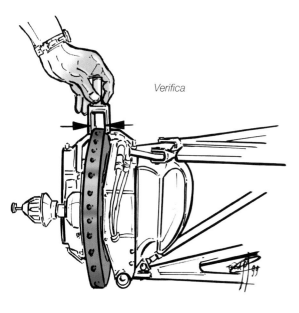

*Verifica*

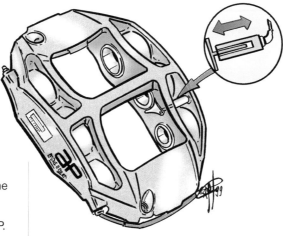

## BRAKE PAD THICKNESS SENSOR

The British firm AP introduced a sensor mounted inside the caliper to detect the state of brake pad wear. The drawing shows the tab in contact with the pads and the small coil (inside the caliper) that detected variations in the magnetic field and thus gauged the thickness of the pad. The '98 season instead saw the introduction of a disc wear sensor.

## DISC THICKNESS VERIFICATION

As in the '98 season, the maximum brake disc thickness was restricted to 28 mm (in '97 thickness reached 34 mm). Shortly before the cars lined up on the grid, a FIA official would use a caliper to check the legality of the discs.

## PROST

John Barnard designed revolutionary master cylinders for Prost (1) located in the lower chassis where they were easily accessed by the mechanics and did not intrude in the area in front of the pedalbox. The drawing shows the version equipped with a spring (2) theoretically prohibited by the regulations and attached to the rocker governing the rear brakes. The first part of the broad brake pedal (3) can also be seen.

## CANADIAN GP

The Canadian GP posed a severe test for braking systems, with more than one driver encountering difficulties due to excessive wear. The most serious episode involved Heinz Harald Frentzen who crashed after the disintegration of a disc (an American Hitco component) on his Jordan. The various teams prepared for the event as best they could, devising special features such as the large air intakes used by Ferrari (see previous page) to cope with the exceptional stresses generated by Montreal's semi-street circuit. There are 6 major braking points with deceleration values over 4 g and peaking at 4.6 g. In just 1.2", in fact the cars pass from 0.8 g positive to 3.8 g negative. In the two most violent braking points they slow from 320 kph to just 120 in 4" with a brake pressure of around 60 bar, or from 300 kph to 80 in 5", while the operating temperatures peak at around 700/800° (average values around 450°).

The table below illustrates the different selections made by the teams on the basis of the variables available: two caliper manufacturers, two disc manufacturers, various kinds of discs, pads and friction surfaces.

## SCHUMACHER'S ACCIDENT
Michael Schumacher's dramatic crash on the first lap of the British GP was due to a leak from the bleed nipple on the left-hand rear caliper, a fault that had already affected other drivers without serious consequences. The increased vibration transmitted by the higher engine speeds of the latest V10s; combined with the stresses deriving from transverse accelerations and riding the kerbs led to mechanical problems with a number of components. From the following Austrian GP, the Ferraris' brake calipers had the bleed nipples locked by a split pin (see page 71).

| Canadian Gran Prix | Disk | | Friction area | |
|---|---|---|---|---|
| | Front | Rear | Front | Rear |
| Ferrari | P6 | P6 | 44 | 44 |
| Benetton | P7 | P7 | 44 | 34 |
| Sauber | P0 | P0 | 44 | 44 |
| Minardi | P0 | P0 | 44 | 44 |
| Jordan | Hitco | Hitco | 44 | 34 |
| Prost | P7 | P0 | 44 | 44 |
| McLaren | Hitco | Hitco | 44 | 44 |
| Stewart | P0 | P0 | 44 | 44 |
| Williams | P7 | P6 | 40 | 34 |
| Arrows | P7 | P7 | 44 | 34 |
| BAR | P7 | P7 | 44 | 34 |

(Brembo: Ferrari through Prost; A+P: McLaren through BAR)

Prost and Jordan only teams to use lighter Brembo calipers, only Jordan fitted with four piston calipers at the back.

## BRAKES TABLE CANADADIAN GP
Brembo offered two 6-pot calipers (stiff and light) and a 4-pot version used on the rear axle only by Jordan. In the AP camp, the teams all opted for the stiffer calipers; there was a smaller version occasionally used at the rear by Williams but not fitted in Canada. The Hitco discs needed lower working temperatures. McLaren used different discs to those fitted to the Jordans. Carbon Industrie offered 4 options: PO, P3, P6 and P7 with the friction coefficient rising along with the number. The P0s were old discs, the PS offered more initial bite, the P6s withstood higher temperatures while remaining fairly stable in terms of wear, while the P7s gave the highest performance but were more critical with a narrow usage range. Ferrari opted for the P6 with pads in a new material that improved their performance. Three types of friction surfaces were used, in some cases differing between front and rear axles for a better thermal balance.

# TYRES 1999

The technical scenario relating to Formula 1 tyres in 1999 was characterised by the monopoly holder Bridgestone's ability to guarantee considerable stability in terms of efficiency, albeit with inferior performance compared with '98 due to two factors:
1°) The FIA's decision to add a fourth groove to the tread of the front tyres matching the rears.
2°) The tyre manufacturer's undertaking not to push technical research in the direction of structural and compound characteristics likely to generate the progress that would undoubtedly be possible despite the new restrictions.

It is therefore worth taking a look at the traditional performance indicator based on percentage increments in lap times compared with those achieved the previous season with cars in qualifying trim. For the sake of convenience, in calculating percentages the signs are inverted so that a positive Δ% represents progress and a negative Δ% regression. Moreover, in the interest of reliability, as well as ignoring the result of the Malaysian GP (a debut race), the non-comparable times from Magny-Cours, the Nürburgring (rain during qualifying), Zeltweg and Monza (wet tracks in 1998) have also been omitted.

As considerable progress was actually made in 1999 in terms of engine and chassis development, the negative influence of tyres on performance was actually even greater. The fourth front groove certainly played an important role as any variation in front end grip significantly upsets the critical balance of the car, both when turning-in (edgy handling and a tendency towards understeer, especially at

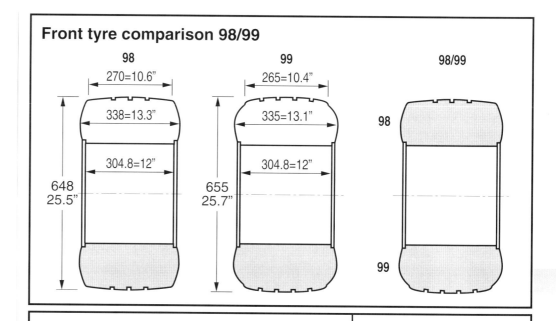

## Front tyre comparison 98/99

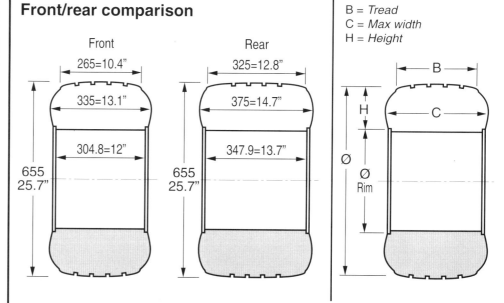

## Front/rear comparison

B = Tread
C = Max width
H = Height

low speeds) and under braking, with the distribution of weight and aerodynamic loading having to be recalibrated. However, this aspect, which may be considered within the ambit of tyre size, was secondary to the gradual passage from harder to softer compounds during the course of the year.

**F**rom the point of view of size, in fact, the Bridgestone front tyre retained the 1998 dimensions with a tread width of 265 mm, despite the generalised use of wheels with 12" rim widths (slight variations were still used) equal to 304.8 mm. The maximum width became 335 mm, while for the first time in the history of Formula 1 the overall diameter of 655 mm was identical to that of the rear tyre (previously the differences had become minimal). Given a tread width of 265 mm we may retain that the contact path (ellipsoidal in shape, with the longer axis equal to the tread width), already reduced by around 16% in 1998 with three grooves, lost around another 7% with the fourth. Compared with the slicks used in the past, in fact, around 23% of the total contact area between tyre and track had been removed, an area that, as is well known, is not directly proportional to grip but strongly influences it. This is particularly true of soft compounds that accentuate the grip of the rubber on the road surface according to a specific rack effect. Rear tyre size remained virtually unchanged with the overall diameter being unified at 655 mm against the previous 659 mm, a tread width of 325 mm and a chord of 375 mm, while the rim was subjected to a barely perceptible increase in width from 13.5 to 13.7" (347.98 mm).

|  | dry | | wet | |
|---|---|---|---|---|
|  | front | rear | front | rear |
| **Marking*** | **265/55R/13** | **325/45R/13** | **245/55R/13** | **325/45R/13** |
| Overall diameter (Ø) | 655 mm | 655 mm | 655 mm | 655 mm |
| Tread | 265 mm | 325 mm | 245 mm | 325 mm |
| Width of section | 335 mm | 375 mm | 325 mm | 375 mm |
| Ø Rim | 12" | 13.7" | 12" | 13.7" |

* **265/55R-13** = (1) Tread - (2) H/C Ratio - (3) R right - (4) Ø Rim

## TYRES STATS

• In its first year as sole supplier Bridgestone took 2,640 tyres to each race, 1,408 drys (8 sets per car with two different compound specifications), 1,232 wets (7 sets, 2 options with the same tread pattern but different compounds), 42 technicians and mechanics and 6/7 engineers. The optimum temperature to which tyres were heated with covers was 80/90°.

• The minimum tyre inflation pressure suggested by Bridgestone was 17.5 psi; in the case of the left-rear blow-out on Hakkinen's McLaren during the German GP the tyre was inflated to 16.3 psi.

• The width of the front wheels at the start of the season reflected the standard size of the '98 season, 12", before passing in mid-season to 12.5", 12.75" and even 13" for qualifying. The most widely used size was however 12.5". Increased camber angles were also used during qualifying.

The tables record the tyre sizes and the identification systems adopted by Bridgestone. At the top is a comparison between the '98 front tyre with three grooves and the '99 version with 4. It can clearly be seen that the contact area diminished and that different tyre shoulder designs were introduced. The second table shows how the front tyres became so wide as to approach the size of the rears. In '98 they were slightly larger but for '99 the FIA introduced maximum width restrictions (355 mm against the 380 mm at the rear).
At the bottom, lastly, Bridgestone's tyre identification system.

| Circuits | Time 1998 (sec) | Time 1999 (sec) | Increment Δ% |
|----------|-----------------|-----------------|--------------|
| Melbourne | 90.010 | 90.462 | -0.50 |
| Interlagos | 77.092 | 76.568 | +0.68 |
| Imola | 85.973 | 86.362 | -0.45 |
| Monte-Carlo | 79.798 | 80.547 | -0.94 |
| Barcellona | 80.262 | 82.088 | -2.28 |
| Montreal | 78.213 | 79.298 | -1.39 |
| Silverstone | 83.720 | 84.804 | -1.29 |
| Hockenheim | 101.838 | 102.950 | -1.09 |
| Budapest | 76.973 | 78.156 | -1.54 |
| Spa | 108.682 | 110.329 | -1.52 |
| Suzuka | 96.293 | 97.470 | -1.22 |
| | | Average | -1.05 |

The '99 season is analysed in these two tables in comparison with the '98 figures. The FIA's aim of slowing the cars was fully achieved, only at one circuit (Interlagos), the cars with 4 grooves were quicker. The second table shows the different track surface conditions, an indispensable factor for understanding the dominant choices the various teams made between the two types of tyres the regulations obliged Bridgestone to offer.

| Circuits | Characteristics | Index I | Km/h(Qual.) | Preferred choice |
|----------|-----------------|---------|-------------|------------------|
| Barcellona | Very abrasive and punishing | 0.6 | 207 | MEDIUM |
| Interlagos | Undulating and fairly abrasive | 0.6 | 202 | MEDIUM |
| Melbourne | Regular and very smooth | 0.5 | 211 | MEDIUM |
| Imola | Slightly abrasive, little grip | 0.5 | 205 | MEDIUM |
| Monza | Hardly abrasive. High speed stress | 0.4 | 252 | MEDIUM |
| Suzuka | Punishing and abrasive | 0.6 | 216 | SOFT |
| Spa | Street-like and abrasive | 0.6 | 227 | SOFT |
| Silverstone | Low roughness, high speed stress | 0.6 | 218 | SOFT |
| Budapest | Averagely abrasive | 0.6 | 183 | SOFT |
| Hockenheim | Polished, high speed stress | 0.5 | 238 | SOFT |
| Nürburgring | Regular and hardly abrasive | 0.5 | 209 | SOFT |
| Magny-Cours | Flat and hardly abrasive | Rain | 200 | SOFT |
| Montreal | Little bumps and hardly abrasive | 0.5 | 201 | SOFT |
| Zeltweg | Very restricted deterioration | 0.4 | 219 | SOFT |
| Monte-Carlo | Street surface with bumps | 0.4 | 151 | SOFT |
| Sepang | Moderately abrasive | 0.5 | 200 | EXTRA-SOFT |

In general terms, the simplified classification drawn up by the Bridgestone technicians with four grades, Extra-Soft, Soft, Medium and Hard, can be seen as a summary of technical and functional characteristics due as much to the radial structure of the tyre as the hysteresis of the rubber, definable as heat produced by unexpressed energy. This means that on the basis of similar results there has been a merging of the 6 types designated in order of increasing hardness: 057/058, 055/056, 061/062, 053/054, 059/060, 051/052 (the first code for the front and the second for the rear tyres). However, the synthesis only reveals the availability of the material on offer at each GP, with the Medium/Soft pair provided for all qualifying sessions except the Monaco and Hungarian GPs, the GP of Europe and the Malaysian GP where the Soft/Extra-Soft pairing was offered, and the Italian GP which required the Hard/Medium option.

For a superficial technical analysis, instead, a key is needed based on the following elements: 1) nature of the track, according to the road surface characteristics and its generation of stress; 2) the speed rating, which also influences rolling resistance; 3) the I index of durability in the first part of the race; 4) the dominant or winning choice. Thus, starting with the hardest tyres it will be easy to identify (on a chronological basis too), the tendency towards softer grades as the car constructors begin to acquire the ability to get the best out of the 4-groove front tyres.

The Hard option having remained unused, on average between one grade and another differences were recorded such as to guarantee an improvement in lap times in the order of 0.3÷0.4%; only in ideal conditions were improvements of 0.6% achieved. Compared with the Medium option, the Soft and Extra-Soft tyres, frequently less critical when scrubbed, displayed the expected accentuated decay with a very linear progression according to the distance covered. The Medium tyres, with less tread consumption,

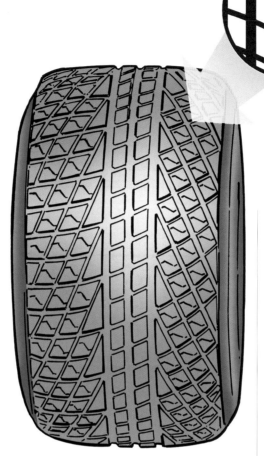

instead showed a clear revival of performance after a certain number of kilometres as a result of the reduction in groove depth and a slight slick-effect. In theory, as we saw with the tyres at the Malaysian GP that allowed the Ferraris to fly, this effect should be repeated with the softer compounds, on the basis of greater knowledge. Given that Bridgestone has demonstrated its great potential in achieving the desired consistency of performance, the next developments could as easily be progressive or asymptotic in order to freeze performance at 1999 levels. At this point, calling into question the regulatory body, it is legitimate to ask whether the technical equilibrium of Formula 1 has not been compromised by the various provisions taken to contain performance: on the one hand engines free to race towards the 900 hp threshold, on the other tyres being continually penalised.

*Enrico Benzing*

## HEAVY RAIN TYRES
For the last race of the season at Suzuka Bridgestone modified its wet weather tyre, introducing a small serpentine incision (highlighted in the circle) to the standard wet tread pattern that had remained unchanged all season, albeit with two different compound options.

# Talking About SUSPENSION

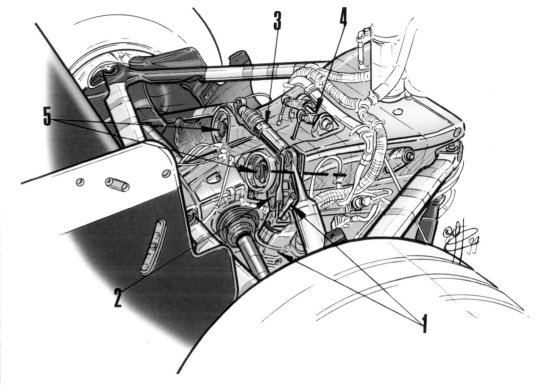

The second season following the prohibition on locating suspension elements within the survival cell saw the establishment of a new trend whereby the majority of the teams followed in the wake of Ferrari and McLaren with the reintroduction of vertical dampers placed in the area in front of the pedalbox combined with vertical push-rod rockers. The old layout with horizontal dampers placed in a niche in the upper part of the chassis (universal up until '97) was retained by two teams only, Jordan and Arrows, although this last also retained the Barnard-designed '98 layout with a unique vertical torsion bar location outside the FIA prohibited zone. Jordan was instead the only team not to use torsion bars on the front axle in '99 (as well as having retained horizontal dampers in the upper chassis), with a layout that was a logical development of the system used in previous seasons. Curiously, whilst McLaren with the new MP4/14 initially abandoned the mid-mounted steering link introduced as a significant innovation in the '98 season (revived from the Australian GP onwards), a fair number of teams (Benetton, Stewart, Sauber, Prost, Minardi and BAR) instead adopted the feature with the link mounted at various points low on the upright. With regards the rear axle, there were a number of very different layouts based on the theme of torsion bars in place of classic coil springs, with Ferrari and Minardi introducing the most interesting new features. McLaren for its part adopted torsion bars at the rear for the first time with a layout inspired by the one designed by Barnard for Arrows in '98 and naturally retained on the '99 car.

## FERRARI

The F399 rear suspension layout was extremely innovative with the classic horizontal damper location above the gearbox being abandoned. Effectively, the layout seen on the front axle in '98 was adopted at the rear too, with a feature that further aided the various adjustment operations performed by the mechanics. 1) The dampers were set vertically either side of the gearbox and linked to the suspension strut via a sophisticated rocker (2) that extended rather than compressed the damper. 3) The third damper or bump stop element was linked to the two rockers, as at the front, and was located above the gearbox. 4) The anti-roll bar was also exposed and easily replaceable. 5) The torsion bars disappeared within the carbonfibre spacer and were slightly inclined with respects to the horizontal plane, a factor that made them easier to replace.

## FERRARI

The F399 was without doubt the car that allowed the various suspension adjustment to be made in the shortest time, with a layout that was very similar front and rear. The drawing shows the replacement of the torsion bars (1) and the regulation of the ride height by means of a screwdriver acting, as at the front, on adjusters placed either side of the gearbox. Turning in a clockwise direction raised the car while an anti-clockwise adjustment lowered it. 3) The replacement of the anti-roll bar and the adjustment of the third bump element (4) was also very rapid.

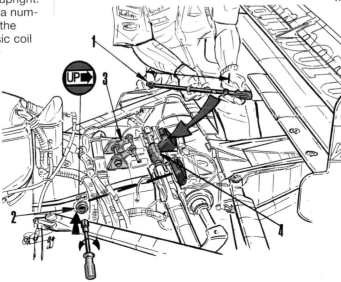

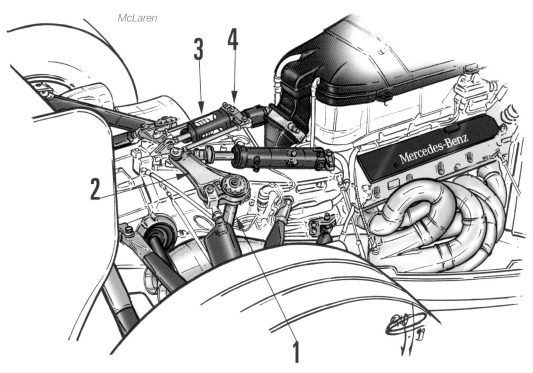

*McLaren*

## McLaREN

McLaren introduced a brand new rear suspension layout featuring for the first time torsion bars in place of coil springs over the dampers (3) which instead remained in the classic location above the gearbox.
1) The torsion bars were mounted

vertically either side of the gearbox in a layout inspired by the one introduced by Barnard on the '98 Arrows. 2) The long rocker providing good suspension travel was retained.
 4) The third bump stop element was linked to the anti-roll bar pivoting within the gearbox.

## McLaREN

With the MP4/14 introduced at the start of the season, McLaren abandoned the upright with a mid-mounted steering link introduced as a significant innovation on the preceding MP4/13, and placed the link inside the aerodynamic upper wishbone. At the Austrian GP, however, the old feature that eliminated production problems and friction generated by the link within the suspension arm was revived.

*Ferrari*

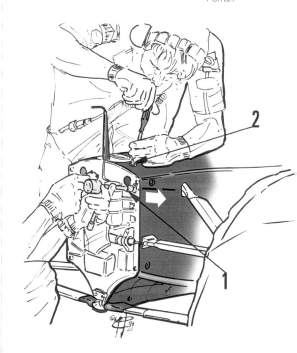

*McLaren*

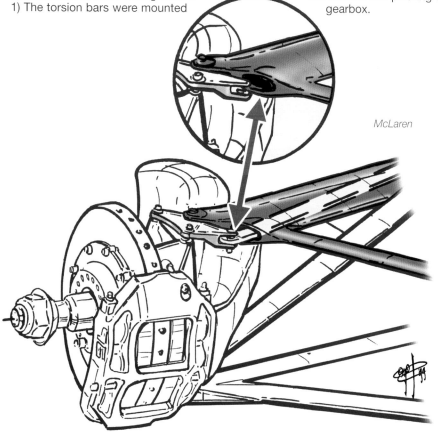

## FERRARI

The front suspension layout of the F399 was virtually unchanged with respects to the old F300, as were the adjustment operations.
1) The extremely simple and rapid removal of the torsion bar was unchanged. 2) Ride height was adjusted with a simple screwdriver acting on exposed pins in the upper part of the chassis linked to a second rocker that acted as a ride height register.

## McLAREN

The McLaren front suspension was also virtually unchanged. The only difference was the completely vertical position of the dampers (1). The arrangement of the horizontal torsion bars (2) and the rockers (3) was instead identical, as was the third damper (4) linked to the anti-roll bar (5). 6) The steering links set within the upper wishbone (on the right in the drawing) at the start of the season, were returned to the lower part of the upright from the Austrian GP onwards, as on the old MP4/13. Note the reduced chassis section highlighted in yellow and by the dotted line.

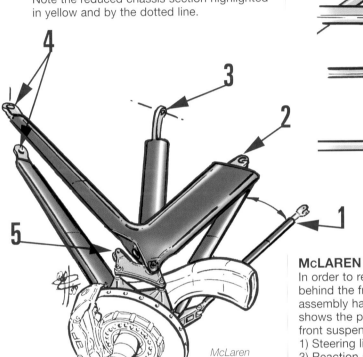

*McLaren*

*McLaren*

## McLAREN

In order to replace the large barge-boards behind the front wheel the whole suspension assembly had to be dismantled. The drawing shows the post-Austrian GP specification front suspension removed from the car.
1) Steering link. 2) Upper wishbone.
3) Reaction arm. 4) Wishbone rear knife-edge mounts. 5) Original steering link mount.

*Jordan*

## BAR

BAR was the only team to have the push rod link mount attached directly to the upright rather than the lower wishbone as on all the other cars. This feature, in vogue on Indy cars, is highlighted in the circle.

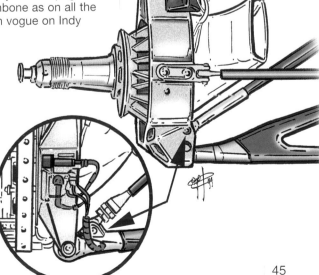

*BAR*

## JORDAN

Jordan was the only team to race a car with horizontal dampers (1) and coaxial coil springs located in niches at the top of the chassis. The layout featured a third bump stop element (2) and an anti-roll bar (3) linked to the rockers (4) still mounted horizontally as on the Arrows. All the other '99 season cars instead featured vertical rockers.

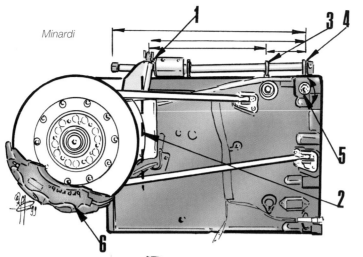

*Minardi*

## MINARDI

Gustav Brunner introduced a very sophisticated rear suspension layout on the Minardi, characterised by very long torsion bars (1) located in the upper part of the gearbox.
2) The dampers were set vertically and concealed within the gearbox. The bars were divided longitudinally by an adjuster (3) allowing the spring rates to be varied beyond a certain degree of compression. 4) At the front end was a second rocker that could be adjusted to vary the ride height (5).
6) The brake caliper was placed low down to lower the centre of gravity of the suspension assembly.

## MINARDI

1) Suspension rockers linked to the damper inside the gearbox and highlighted by the dotted line. 2) The long torsion bars had two further adjusters (3-4) to vary the spring rate. 5) The roll-bar was articulated like the one fitted to the front axle of the Ferrari.

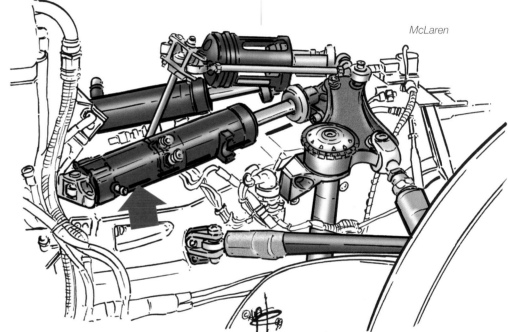

*McLaren*

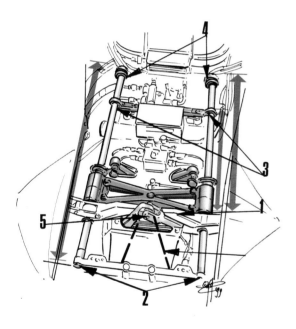

## FERRARI

At Monaco all teams strengthen the suspension mounts and the steering links (1) (the standard version is seen alongside).
2) The wishbones are also modified to prevent them being fouled by the wheels given that the steering angle is increased (to 22°).
3) Larger brake air intakes.

## McLAREN

From the Canadian GP onwards the McLarens were fitted with a third bump stop element as at the front and like the previous season's car. It was linked to the long rockers and the anti-roll bar. Note the absence of the potentiometers which were removed for the race to save weight.

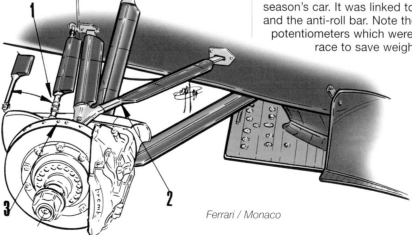

*Ferrari / Monaco*

## BENETTON

Benetton adopted a third bump stop element located horizontally between the two suspension rockers, a feature introduced by Ferrari in '98 and retained on the F399.

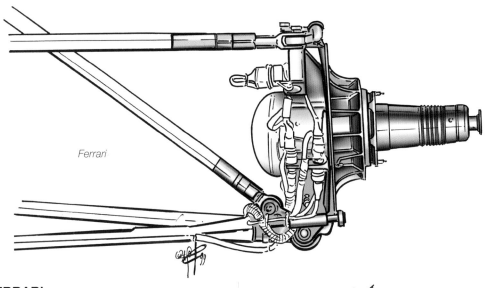

*Ferrari*

## FERRARI

The Ferrari front upright in fabricated titanium was very sophisticated. Note the cooling vanes in the central section and the various brake disc temperature (top) and thickness (bottom) sensors.

## STEWART

The shape of the upper front wishbone on the Stewart was unusual. The wing profile (with a notable chord) slopes conspicuously backwards, highlighted in the top drawing. Stewart was one of the teams that followed McLaren's lead with the MP4/13 in mounting the steering link lower down, albeit not in the middle of the upright.

## WILLIAMS

Williams was one of the few teams (together with Jordan and BAR) to retain classic coil-over dampers (1) rather than adopting torsion bars. The very short anti-roll bar (2) was mounted above the rockers. Note that in place of the triangular upper wishbone is a quadrilateral design.

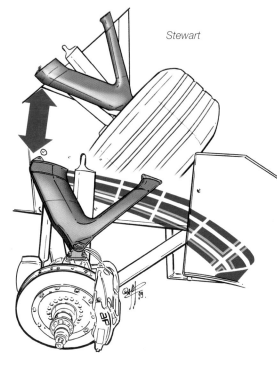

*Stewart*

*Williams*

*Camber*

## CAMBER

For qualifying most teams increased the camber angle by half a degree to increase the efficiency of the Bridgestone tyres. The drawing shows the replacement of the small connecting plate on the upright that allows this adjustment.

# Talking about DOWNFORCE

This was a very demanding season for the various teams' aerodynamicists. In the wake of the severe restrictions introduced in '98 (the wheels set 10 cm closer either side of the car requiring a true revolution in the study of the air flows) they had to cope with further limitations of the efficiency of the front tyres with the addition of the fourth groove which made the attainment of satisfactory aerodynamic balance that much more difficult. There were no major innovations in the field following the numerous interesting experiments introduced by even the so-called minor teams in that first season of narrow tracks and grooved tyres. There was a general adoption of certain trends that emerged at the end of '98 such as the alignment of the front wing end-plates with the tyres and greater attention paid to the air flow in the central section of the car where a number of teams followed McLaren's lead with a low nose and a V-shaped section at the front of the chassis (see Stewart). As much work as possible was done on improving aerodynamic efficiency (the ratio between the downforce and drag coeffi-

cients), concentrating on the reduction of frontal area. The designers were trying above all to achieve good loading stability so as not to compromise braking into and traction out of corners, delicate phases already penalised by the reduced grip of the four-groove tyres and harder compounds. In order to achieve optimum aerodynamic efficiency, designers sought to reduce to a minimum variations in balance and loading with respects to ride height by means of increasing ground clearance as much as possible. In this way they attempted to recover grip through greater suspension travel and the possibility of using softer springs. There were two surprises among the range of aerodynamic features employed in '99. The first was the use of delta-shaped wings by Ferrari at the rear too, although only at the two ultra-fast tracks, Hockenheim and Monza. At the front a similar feature had been introduced at the Nürburgring in '98 and retained at all the circuits in '99. A welcome return to the past given that this type of wing had already been used on the 312 B3, T, T2, T3, T4, T5 and 126 C in the Seventies, a fea-

|  | Cz | Cx | Eff. | S. km/h | D. kg |
|---|---|---|---|---|---|
| **Australia** | 2.496 | 0.981 | 2.54 | 297 | 1442 |
| **Brazil** | 2.511 | 0.942 | 2.67 | 305 | 1530 |
| **San Marino** | 2.421 | 0.912 | 2.65 | 306 | 1470 |
| **Monaco** | 2.661 | 1.000 | 2.66 | 290 | 1478 |
| **Spain** | 2.447 | 0.898 | 2.72 | 305 | 1516 |
| **Canada** | 2.257 | 0.832 | 2.71 | 319 | 1504 |
| **France** | 2.628 | 0.962 | 2.73 | 297 | 1520 |
| **G.Britain** | 2.436 | 0.872 | 2.79 | 310 | 1533 |
| **Austria** | 2.330 | 0.884 | 2.64 | 306 | 1429 |
| **Germany** | 1.908 | 0.697 | 2.74 | 345 | 1455 |
| **Hungary** | 2.647 | 0.990 | 2.67 | 300 | 1561 |
| **Belgium** | 2.418 | 0.850 | 2.84 | 315 | 1572 |
| **Italy** | 1.845 | 0.680 | 2.71 | 347 | 1435 |
| **Europe** | 2.586 | 0.938 | 2.76 | 305 | 1576 |
| **Malaysia** | 2.580 | 0.952 | 2.71 | 304 | 1562 |
| **Japan** | 2.633 | 0.991 | 2.66 | 300 | 1552 |

Values for average 750 HP car

**Cz** = Downforce coefficient
**Cx** = Drag coefficient
**Eff.** = Efficiency
**S** = Speed
**D** = Downforce

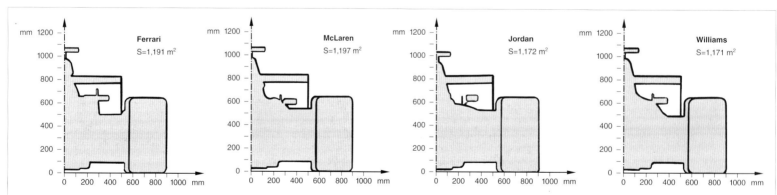

## HOCKENHEIM '99
Comparison of the frontal areas used on the ultra-fast Hockenheim track helps to explain why Williams and Jordan were so competitive. They were in fact the two cars with the smallest frontal area thanks to the shape of their side-pods (very low on the Williams with protec-

tions either side of the cockpit virtually non-existent on the Jordan) and the use of smaller rear wings, especially with respects to the McLaren whose frontal area was also greater than that of the Ferrari.

ture requested by Ing. Mauro Forghieri but actually created by an enthusiastic modeller, «Chichi» Guglielminetti. The debut of the B3 in the 1973 Austrian GP created a sensation but the delta wing then became something of a tradition for Maranello's cars up to the end

of the decade. The second surprise came from Jordan which in Hungary revived the third advanced winglet (introduced by McLaren in '95) when we all thought that it had been definitively outlawed by the restrictions imposed by the FIA. The table docu-

ments the immense amount of development work conducted by the aerodynamicists in order to try to improve the efficiency of the cars with a general reduction of the Cx value with respects to those recorded in the analysis of the '98 season.

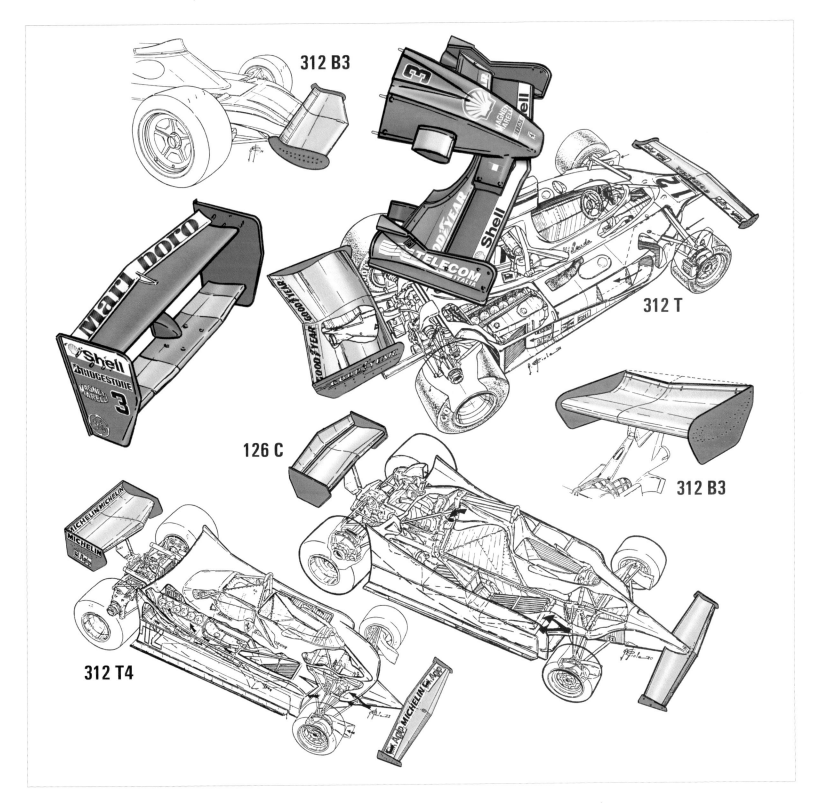

## JORDAN HUNGARY

At Budapest, where there was a frantic search for maximum downforce, even at the expense of efficiency, Jordan exploited a loophole in the regulations regarding the area between the roll bar and the 103 cm from the rear axle and dusted off the idea of the 3rd advanced winglet (introduced by McLaren in '95) out-lawed by the severe FIA restrictions. The pro-hibited area is highlighted in red in this draw-ing. The chord of the 60-cm wide winglet was thus 30 cm.

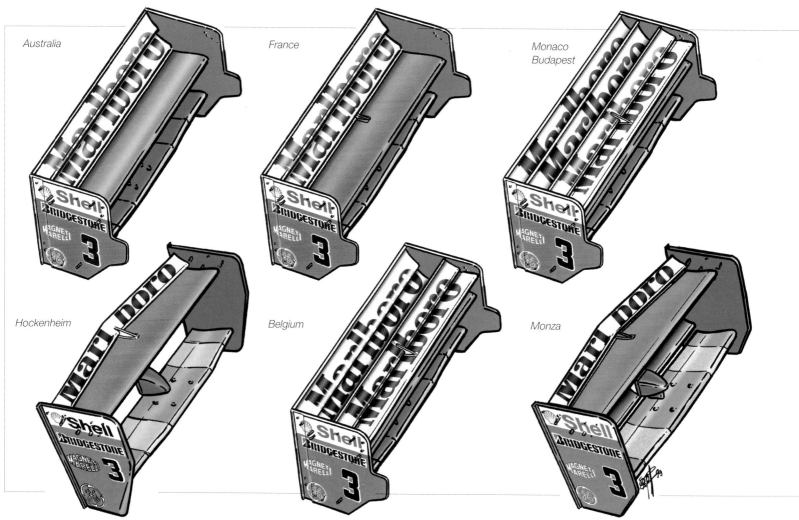

Australia

France

Monaco
Budapest

Hockenheim

Belgium

Monza

## FERRARI WINGS

The major difference in the rear wings used by Ferrari in '99 was the return to the reversed delta shape on the ultra-fast Hock-enheim and Monza tracks. Note the further refinement at Monza with a different tail light location with respects to the lower plane (a modification also made to the other wings but not visible in the drawings). Monza also saw the use of a high downforce version of the wing equipped with different end-plates and a flap on the lower section of the main-plane. Considerable work was done to optimise the position of the various profiles, with the use of elements of varying shapes and chords notable on the first two wings. On high down-force tracks two types of wings were used with a variable number of planes, the most being employed at Monaco and Budapest of course. The inverted-U lower planes in the central section seen in '98 were abandoned.

## McLAREN

In effect McLaren used two rear wing designs. On the left is depicted the slow track version with dual planes to the front at the top and a second flap in the lower section with raised planes in the centre. On the right, the version for ultra-fast tracks with a single plane at the bottom and two elements with reduced chords at the top.

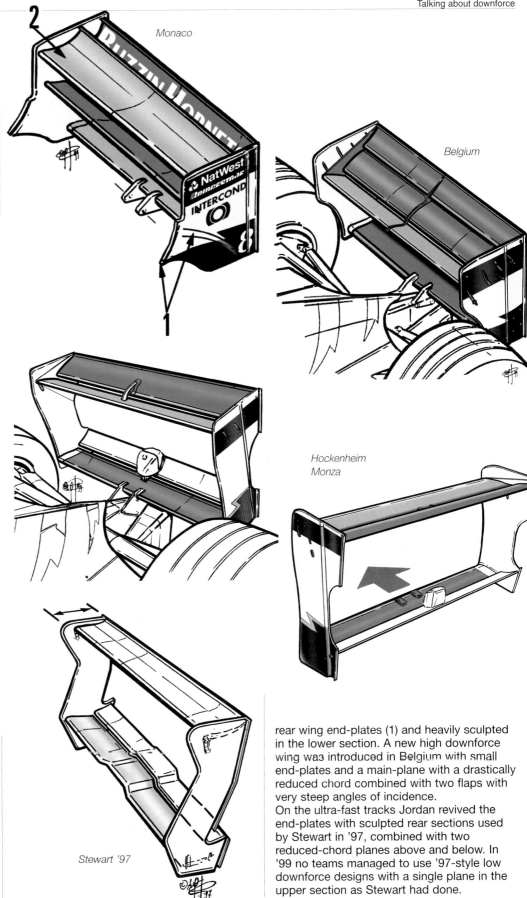

*Monaco*

*Belgium*

*Hockenheim Monza*

*Stewart '97*

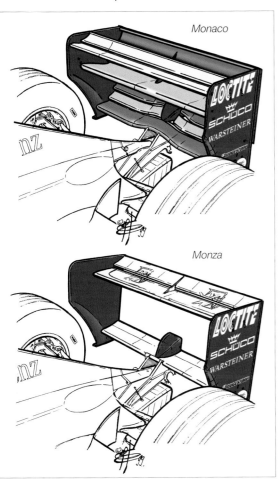

*Monaco*

*Monza*

## JORDAN

Jordan was one of the teams that introduced new ideas in the field of wing design. On the left can be seen the high downforce wing derived from the one introduced at Monaco and featuring a large main-plane surmounted by a single (2) plane with a notable chord in place of the two elements highlighted in the drawing of the McLaren (a design almost universally adopted in '99). Note that on the medium-slow tracks Jordan used bodywork equipped with long extensions linked to the rear wing end-plates (1) and heavily sculpted in the lower section. A new high downforce wing was introduced in Belgium with small end-plates and a main-plane with a drastically reduced chord combined with two flaps with very steep angles of incidence.

On the ultra-fast tracks Jordan revived the end-plates with sculpted rear sections used by Stewart in '97, combined with two reduced-chord planes above and below. In '99 no teams managed to use '97-style low downforce designs with a single plane in the upper section as Stewart had done.

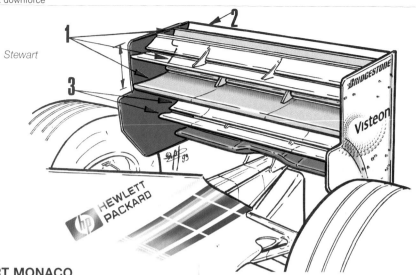

*Stewart*

*Prost Monza*

*Prost Belgium*

## STEWART MONACO

Stewart introduced a rear wing at Monaco with the main section (plane and two flaps) (2) surmounted by two additional advanced planes (3) above the lower plane.

## FERRARI HIGH DOWNFORCE

This drawing depicts the various elements of the wings used with diverse combinations according to the demands of the high downforce tracks. There were two main-plane options (1), the first with a shorter chord (fitted to the car) and a longer chord combined with a flap (2) in an intermediate position with respects to the dual flap on the leading edge (always fitted on slow tracks), the second with two planes (2) behind the main flaps. A further plane could be mounted above these two on the wing strut itself. Note that at Monaco (in the circle) the new bodywork with a small tab in front of the wheels had yet to be introduced

## PROST

The main-plane noted in the version used in Belgium was very new. It first appeared, however, at Monaco where the concave element was of course concealed by the planes added to the upper section. Note the long lateral Gurney flap extending to the lower part of the end-plate.

On the fast circuits of Hockenheim and Monza, Prost opted from two very narrow chord profiles above and below (2) rather than the extreme solutions seen in the previous two years. There were, however, new end-plates (1) with a sinuous shape to the front part and two small vertical Gurney flaps at the rear (3).

## FERRARI
## FRONTAL AREA COMPARISON

A comparison of the frontal area of the F399 in the two extreme configurations (Hockenheim on the left and Monaco on the right). The front wing flaps were different as, above all, were the elements of the rear wing that increase the Cx from about 0.65 to 1.0. It is easy to see how drag increased with such a larger frontal area as shown in the configuration on the right.

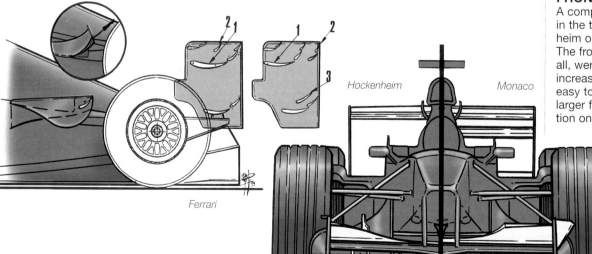

*Ferrari*

*Hockenheim*

*Monaco*

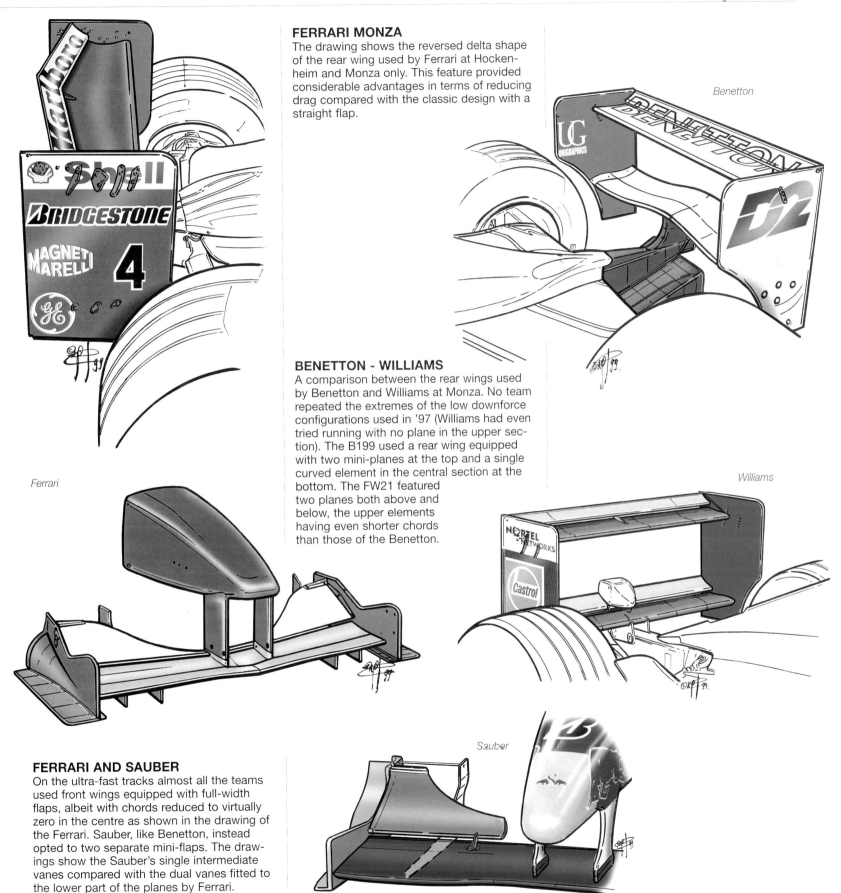

## FERRARI MONZA

The drawing shows the reversed delta shape of the rear wing used by Ferrari at Hockenheim and Monza only. This feature provided considerable advantages in terms of reducing drag compared with the classic design with a straight flap.

*Benetton*

## BENETTON - WILLIAMS

A comparison between the rear wings used by Benetton and Williams at Monza. No team repeated the extremes of the low downforce configurations used in '97 (Williams had even tried running with no plane in the upper section). The B199 used a rear wing equipped with two mini-planes at the top and a single curved element in the central section at the bottom. The FW21 featured two planes both above and below, the upper elements having even shorter chords than those of the Benetton.

*Ferrari*

*Williams*

*Sauber*

## FERRARI AND SAUBER

On the ultra-fast tracks almost all the teams used front wings equipped with full-width flaps, albeit with chords reduced to virtually zero in the centre as shown in the drawing of the Ferrari. Sauber, like Benetton, instead opted to two separate mini-flaps. The drawings show the Sauber's single intermediate vanes compared with the dual vanes fitted to the lower part of the planes by Ferrari.

# Talking about UNDERBODIES

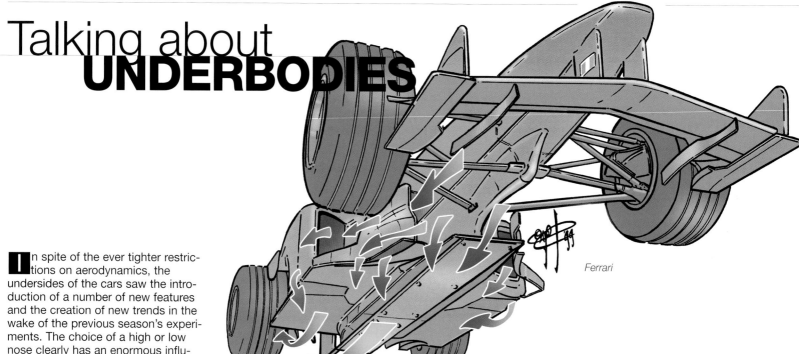

*Ferrari*

In spite of the ever tighter restrictions on aerodynamics, the undersides of the cars saw the introduction of a number of new features and the creation of new trends in the wake of the previous season's experiments. The choice of a high or low nose clearly has an enormous influence on the air flow across the underbody and thus on the shape of diffuser profiles. The 1999 World Championship field was divided into two groups with Ferrari, Williams, Benetton, Sauber, Minardi and Arrows opting to try to channel as much air as possible by using variations on the high nose and flat underbody theme. In the drawing of the Ferrari from below it can be seen that the large central fin acting as the lower wishbone mount in the area behind the front wing also directed the air flow towards the lower part of the side-pods and the rear of the car. This last area was also directly influenced by another choice that divided the teams: the position of the exhausts that with their blowing severely affect the quality of the air flow. The majority of the cars featured the more «traditional» layout; that is to say, with the exhausts located immediately above the lateral channels. The two exceptions were Williams, who introduced the idea of exhausts blowing in the lower part of the central tunnel, and Ferrari who retained the high exhausts introduced at the Spanish GP in '98. At the Belgian GP another two teams (Stewart and Prost) followed Maranello's suite, thus creating a fairly substantial group of cars with high exhausts for the first season of the new Millennium. Apart from this initial differentiation, most teams presented underbodies representing logical evolutions of the choices made in the '98 season with no major innovations. The objective of the aerodynamic testing conducted in the wind tunnels was that of creating a car with underbody aerodynamics that were less critical with regards to variations in ride height so as to be able to count on accentuated suspension efficiency and to contain the negative effects

associated with the reduced grip provided by the front tyres with 4 grooves and the harder compound imposed by the FIA. The only new features were restricted to the area of the seal between the rear wheels documented in this chapter and on page 29 (New Features chapter) A plane was iontroduced in front of the wheels on the uncompetitive Benetton B199 with the aim of better sealing this delicate area, the source of notable turbulence detrimental to the quality of the air flow.

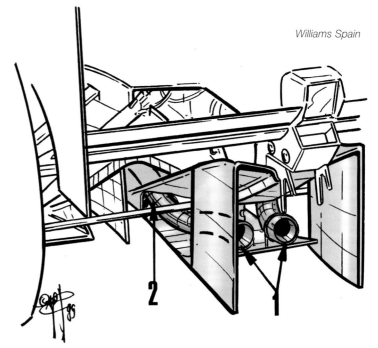

*Williams Spain*

54

## WILLIAMS

Williams lined up with the FW21 designed by Gavin Fisher and Geoff Willis and featuring new exhausts blowing low in the central tunnel. Early in the year very short exhaust pipes semi-concealed by the fairings were seen while at the Spanish GP instead a much longer version (2) of the system meant that the exhausts were exposed at the end of the lower horizontal plane (1) of the central tunnel. The package of substantial modifications introduced at the British GP also included the elimination of the central exhaust.

*Ferrari Hockenheim*

## FERRARI AND WILLIAMS

Ferrari introduced further trickery in the form of a diffuser designed specifically for the ultra-fast tracks and thus used at Hockenheim and Monza only. It featured a modification to the flat plane sealing the lateral channels from the inside of the wheels, imitating a similar feature introduced by Williams at the San Marino GP. The new feature is highlighted by the circle on the right in the view of the F399 from below, while in the drawing of the Williams it is the detail at the bottom. In practice, the horizontal knife-edge plane was raised by 3-4 cm, creating a kind of mini-tunnel composed of two small vertical walls in the lower part where there was originally a small vertical fin in the upper part. Williams instead used this feature on all circuits.

*Williams San Marino*

## BALLAST

One of the major technical themes of the season was the increasingly widespread use of ballast (with upwards of 70 kg being employed in some cases) by almost all the teams in order to try to optimise weight distribution according the track characteristics. A loop-hole in the regulations allowed this ballast to be placed within the wooden board on the underside of the car where it thus had the additional benefit of lowering the centre of gravity and thus reducing the lateral loading shifts that had become more critical when narrower track widths were imposed. The first team to introduce this new feature using extremely expensive tungsten bars was Williams in the final races of the '98 season; Ferrari had instead introduced ballast plaques in the upper part of the knife-edge zone as early as the Austrian GP of '97. The feature was retained and is revealed by the holes bored in the knife-edge seen in the drawing of the Williams (1). In addition plaques were applied to the lower sections, as seen in the drawing of the McLaren. These plaques were the centre of considerable controversy when those fitted to the Ferrari and the Stewart

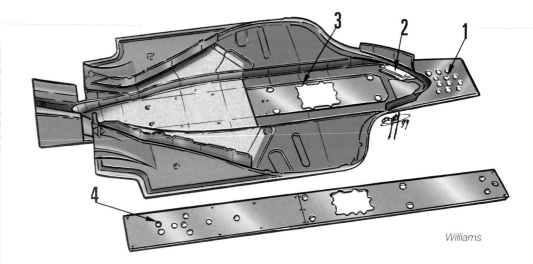

*Williams*

were examined and were found to be flush with the wooden board rather than internal as required by the regulations. The Ferrari was examined on the Thursday and was thus able to modify the feature in time for qualifying, but Stewart's infraction was discovered only

*Ferrari '97*

after the race and consequently led to the disqualification of Herbert. The other great advantage of the external location in the wooden board was that the mechanics could vary the weight distribution without dismantling the underbody as in the case of the Williams (2) fitted with both internal and external ballast with plaques (2) and inserts (4) fitted in addition to the 10 titanium slides introduced by the FIA at Suzuka in '95. These slides were intended to avoid disqualification due to the excessive wear (10% in weight and thickness) of the 1 cm thick wooden board caused by contact with the kerbs.

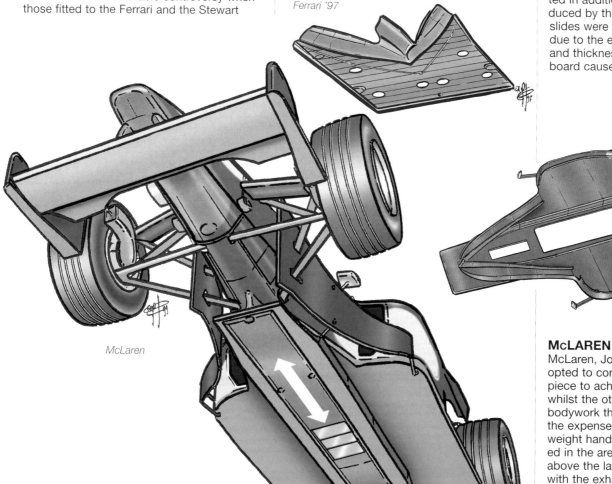

*McLaren*

*McLaren*

## McLAREN

McLaren, Jordan, Williams and Benetton opted to construct their underbodies in one piece to achieve greater torsional stiffness, whilst the other teams preferred two-piece bodywork that was more easily modified at the expense of less rigidity and a slight weight handicap. The small vertical fins located in the area inside the rear wheels and above the lateral channels in correspondence with the exhausts are highlighted in yellow.

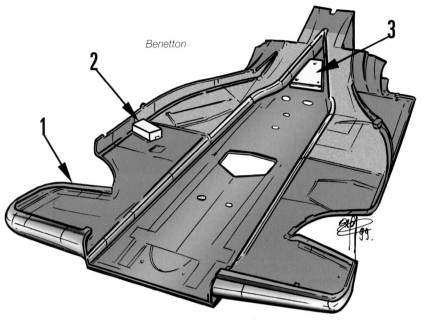

*Benetton*

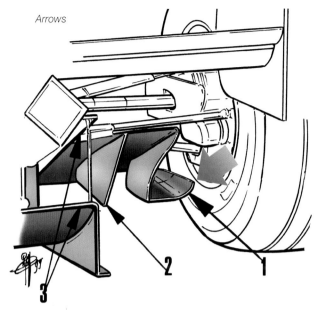

*Arrows*

## BENETTON

The underbody of the Benetton comprised not only the stepped bottom, but also the fairings (1) covering the protection structures in the areas in front of the side-pods. The obligatory 5 kg ballast (2) compensating the installation of video equipment on the camera-car and the ballast placed by the team at the rear to vary the weight distribution (3) are highlighted in the drawing. A different forward location in the knife-edge zone is shown in the Benetton chapter on page 101.

## FERRARI

Ferrari continued to use the two-piece stepped bottom with a design very similar to that employed in the '98 season. Two-piece underbodies were also used by Stewart, Prost, Sauber, Minardi, Arrows and BAR. The version used at Hockenheim and Monza, with the part sealing the rear wheels raised to form a further mini-channel, is highlighted in the circle.

## ARROWS

One of the few innovations in the field of underbodies was introduced by Arrows: in combination with a dual central tunnel (3), the bottom section of which very low, there was a single inclined medial vane (2) and above all a new shape for the horizontal plane sealing the rear wheel (1) In place of the vertical fin used by many teams, Arrows presented a lip curving sharply upwards, highlighted by the red arrow.

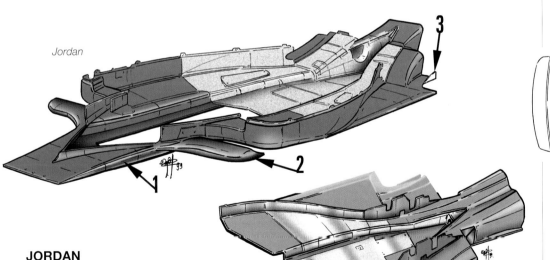

*Jordan*

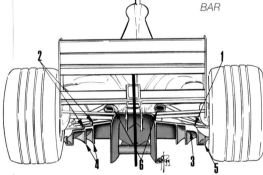

*Ferrari*

*BAR*

## JORDAN

Jordan's underbody was derived from that of the previous season's car and retained the convex section (1) in the usually flat knife-edge zone. New fairings were introduced in front of the side-pod intakes (2) at the Spanish GP. Jordan was the first team to introduce these vertical fins (3) in '97, imitated in that season only by Ferrari but subsequently by many other teams.

## BAR

The BAR was the only '99 car to use dual medial vanes for each lateral channel (4). Diverse designs and sections were used for the mini-channels as can be seen in the comparison with the rear aerodynamic package introduced at the Austrian GP (on the right in the drawing), in which the upper part of the lateral channel (1) was rounded, the steps visible on the left (2) having been eliminated. The height of the mini-channels was also different with the external one divided in height (3). It should be noted that both versions featured a small vertical shield inside the wheels (5).

# Talking About **NOSES**

The design of the F1 nose with its full complement of elements such as wings, relative ground clearance, end-plates and their position with respects to the wheels, is capable of influencing the aerodynamic package of the car as a whole. The narrower tracks introduced by the FIA for the '98 season completely revolutionised one of the fundamental parameters, that of the position of the end-plates with respects to the tyres. In the '98 season, after a very lively period that saw a host of different solutions and approaches to the problem, a generalised trend emerged with the end-plates realigned inside the tyres to improve the quality of the air flow towards the centre of the car. Most teams preferred not to exploit the full width available for the wings (fixed at 140 cm by the regulations) to prevent the airflow striking the tyres that were 10 cm closer to the car either side. Interestingly, in this phase of development, new features were proposed not only

by the leading teams but also those considered to be in the second division such as Tyrrell, Arrows and Minardi who were the first to reposition the endplates further inboard, with horizontal and vertical planes extending from 6 to 10 cm on the outside. The front-end designs of the '99 cars were thus the logical evolution of the experiments carried out in the first season with narrow tracks. The range of new solutions was inevitably restricted with the various teams falling into line with the trend of wings reduced to a little over 120 cm in width and generous (and more or less elaborate) end-plates. McLaren was the exception in retaining wings with full-width leading edges but narrower trailing edges in front of the wheels. McLaren and Williams were the only teams not to use intermediate vanes on the undersides of the wings, evidence of superior aerodynamic compromises in terms of air flow quality below the front wing. The collection of new features tested and docu-

mented in this chapter is therefore less rich than the '98 season's with the difference immediately apparent in the case of Ferrari. In '98 we were accustomed to seeing Maranello's cars with highly individual noses with diverse wing and end-plate configurations for each race. Seven different noses were used to suit the diverse characteristics of the circuits against the 4 employed in '99. A trend was set by the feature introduced at the Luxembourg GP in '98 with V-shaped front wing, the standard version with a rectangular plan being abandoned for the rest of the season. with regards the end-plates too, those seen in '99 were evolutions of the ones introduced at the Nürburgring, with a convex section on the outside and a concave central area. A V-shaped front wing was used in every race. The variations came in the section of the wing, the form of the flaps, the end-plates and the position and number of intermediate vanes.

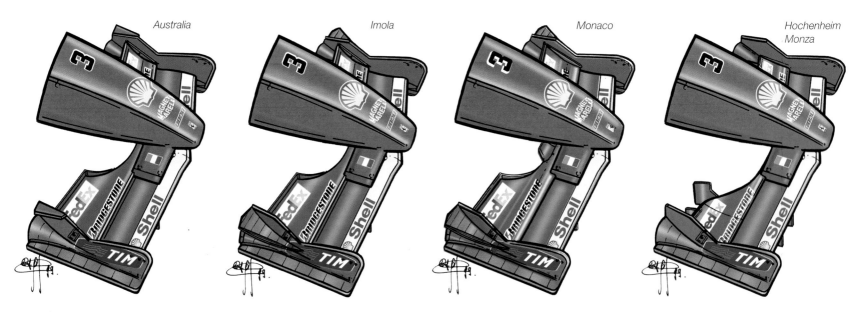

*Australia*

*Imola*

*Monaco*

*Hochenheim*
*Monza*

## FERRARI

Throughout the season Ferrari used V-shaped front wings deriving from the one introduced for the last 3 races of the '98 season. This was particularly innovative on the very fast tracks of Hockenheim and Monza where rectangular-plan wings had always been used in the past. As can be seen in the view from above, Maranello went down a different route to its rival McLaren, using wings reduced to around 120 cm in width in order to realign the end-plates in relation to the tyres which had been brought 10 cm closer to the body of the car either side. This feature had already been used in '98. The drawing compares the maximum download version, left, with the light download alternative, right, used at Hockenheim and Monza only. The main planes were always V-shaped. Both designs belonged to the family introduced at the San Marino GP with the rear section slightly concave, albeit with a different chord. All the components in the wing assembly were different starting with the end-plates which shared only the external concave section, covered by a conspicuous fin in the high downforce version, left. The end-plates were even more highly differentiated when seen from below, with the presence of two intermediate vanes in place of the single element fitted to the low downforce version, right, combined with a reduced chord main plane. The reduction of the flap in the central section was so extreme it virtually ceased to exist. On the left can be seen the larger flap used on slow tracks such as Monaco. The size and shape of the Gurney flaps at the sides of the spoon-shaped extension in the central zone were different.

At the bottom can instead be seen the sequence of wings used during the season. The first is the one used in Austria and Brazil and equipped with end-plates and a main plane similar to the one used in the last races of '98. The second was introduced at Imola and equipped with new end-plates (to which were added a new external fin fitted with a small lateral Gurney flap) and a different family of main planes with a concave trailing edge. This wing was used with various flap configurations on almost all the tracks with the exception of those requiring high downforce and the super-fast Hockenheim and Monza. The slow track nose was derived from this version, with larger flaps, taller lower vanes and spoon-shaped appendages in the central zone. The last nose was used for the super-fast tracks, with simplified end-plates, main plane and flaps with very restricted chords and double intermediate vanes, the central one very tall towards the rear.

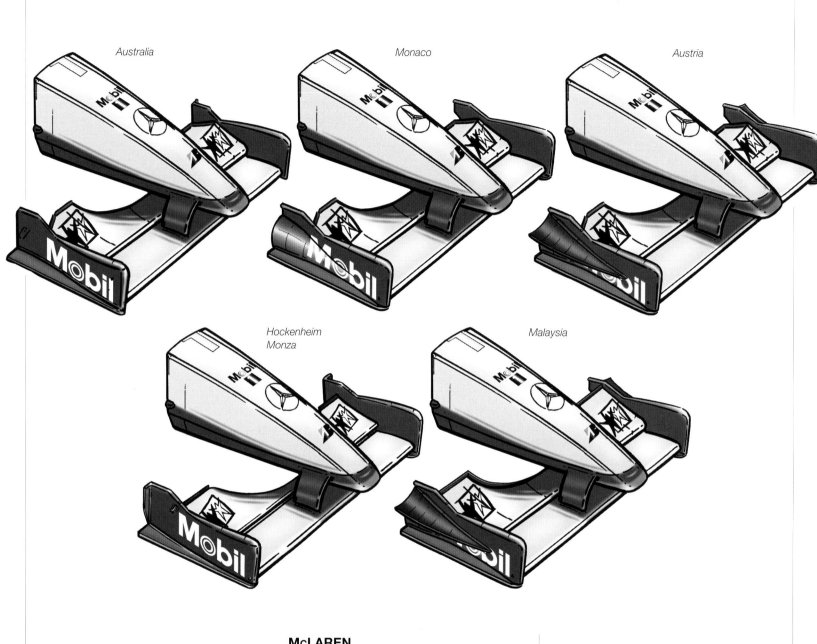

Australia

Monaco

Austria

Hockenheim
Monza

Malaysia

## McLAREN

McLaren displayed very coherent thinking with the philosophy of full-width wings and end-plates derived from the previous season. The principal differences were the introduction of a new main wing profile and the evolution of the end-plates introduced at Suzuka the previous year. The main difference with respects to the McLaren front-end of '98 lay in the fact that the MP4/14 had a considerably longer and slightly slimmer nose thanks to the setting back of the survival cell's front bulkhead which allowed the central section between the wheels to be narrowed. In the sequence of noses that equipped the '98 McLaren, the version that opened the championship had straight side-walls curving inwards at the rear combined with more or less square flaps. The second version featured end-plates equipped with a convex section on the outside that acted as the base for a new element introduced at the Austrian GP and comprising a conspicuous fin bent outwards. There was a further evolution in the last two races with a larger, squarer flap. On fast tracks recourse was made to a design used the previous season with straight end-plates and flaps with a very short chord, above all in the central area, and equipped with a small Gurney flap.

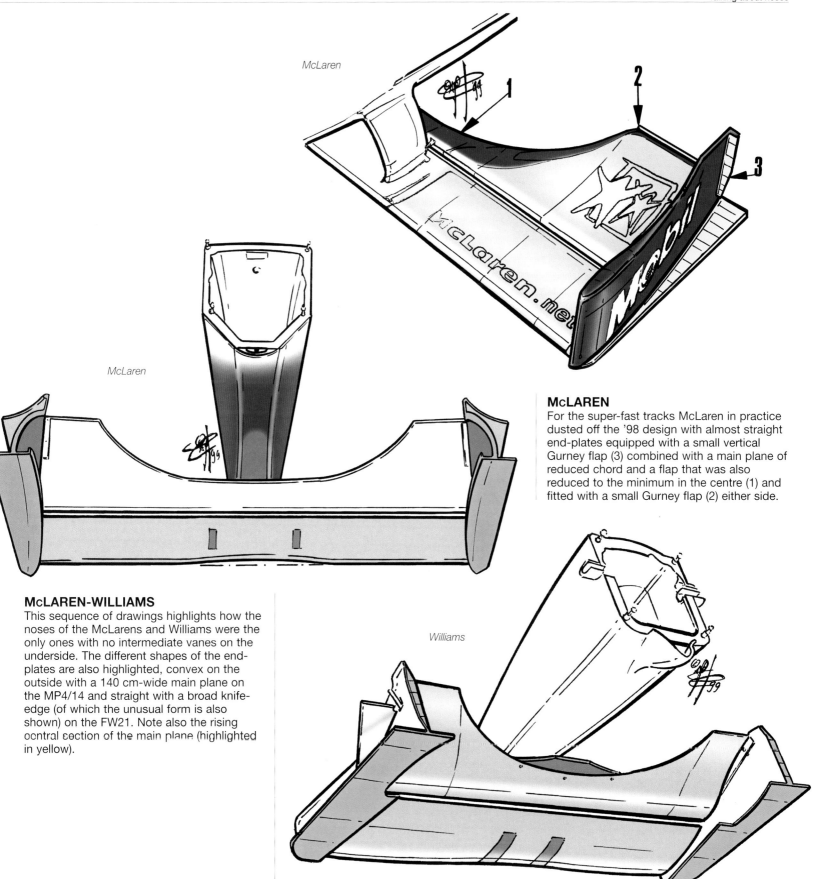

*McLaren*

*McLaren*

## McLAREN

For the super-fast tracks McLaren in practice dusted off the '98 design with almost straight end-plates equipped with a small vertical Gurney flap (3) combined with a main plane of reduced chord and a flap that was also reduced to the minimum in the centre (1) and fitted with a small Gurney flap (2) either side.

## McLAREN-WILLIAMS

This sequence of drawings highlights how the noses of the McLarens and Williams were the only ones with no intermediate vanes on the underside. The different shapes of the end-plates are also highlighted, convex on the outside with a 140 cm-wide main plane on the MP4/14 and straight with a broad knife-edge (of which the unusual form is also shown) on the FW21. Note also the rising central section of the main plane (highlighted in yellow).

*Williams*

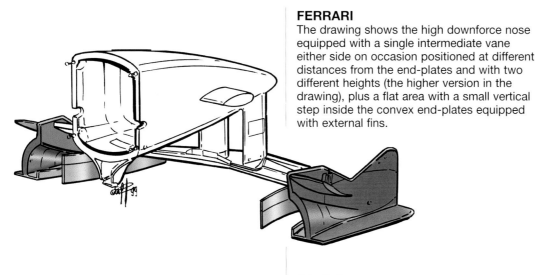

## FERRARI

The drawing shows the high downforce nose equipped with a single intermediate vane either side on occasion positioned at different distances from the end-plates and with two different heights (the higher version in the drawing), plus a flat area with a small vertical step inside the convex end-plates equipped with external fins.

## SAUBER

Sauber retained as in the previous season skewed and very tall intermediate vanes beyond the main planes. The Swiss team also drastically reduced the maximum width of the wings so as to adopt end-plates aligned with the more inboard positioning of the tyres.

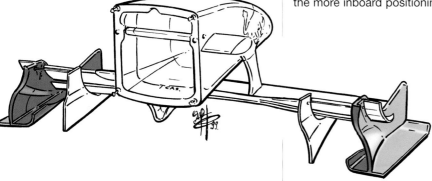

## STEWART

Stewart began the season with the large intermediate vanes introduced at the Austrian GP in '98 and small horizontal planes located halfway up the end-plates, later copied by Minardi. From the French GP the large intermediate vanes were eliminated.

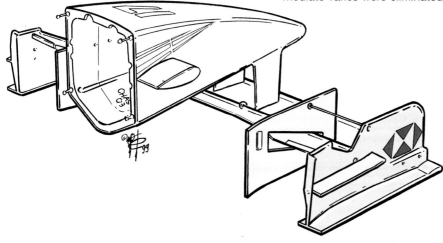

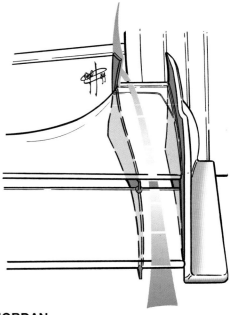

## JORDAN

Jordan used very different intermediate vanes, both in terms of their location close to the end-plates and above all their shape. They were in fact curved inwards, in contrast to those used by the rest of the teams. The aim was still that of optimising air flow across the lower part of the car.

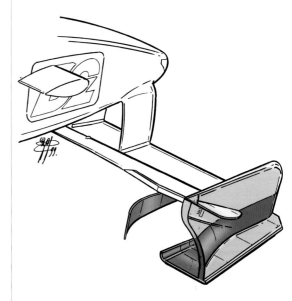

## BENETTON

Benetton too used an intermediate vane on the underside of the main plane notably curved outwards to better separate the flow of air from the turbulence created by the wheels. The drawing shows the end-plate used before Monza equipped with straight vanes at the top and a full-width flap.

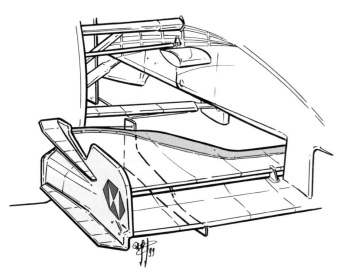

## STEWART

New front end-plates for the Stewarts, in line with the general trend of a convex external area and triangular fins. The large intermediate vanes were also changed in favour of vanes projecting slightly at the rear beyond the full-width flap equipped with an extension (highlighted in grey) on tracks requiring high downforce.

## BAR

The BAR's front wing was very different with end-plates brought in towards the centre and equipped with a wing profile (in yellow). The large, full-width flap had an unusual sinuous form and was, of course, used on tracks requiring high downforce.

## BENETTON

At Monza Benetton used a different front wing with respects to the one used a month earlier on the fast Hockenheim track (left in the drawing). The end-plates were cut away in the mid-section and the convex element was surmounted by a triangular fin abandoned by most other teams at Monza. Together with Sauber, Benetton was one of the only teams to use the double flaps seen in '98 on the Williams and Prost too.

## MINARDI

The drawing shows the new nose introduced at Imola. The wing struts sloped forwards to take into account the lengthening of the wheelbase obtained by inclining the front suspension arms. The two end-plates introduced during the season are separately highlighted. Both were cut away in the central section and equipped with a Stewart-type horizontal plane for use on tracks requiring high downforce.

## PROST

Prost experimented with various nose designs; the version illustrated here was very different in the concave shape of the endplates where the other teams instead opted for external convexities. Note the large flap equipped with a large Gurney flap and the presence of two intermediate vanes, the central one of which was higher in the part beyond the wing profiles.

# The secrets of the
# TWO RIVALS

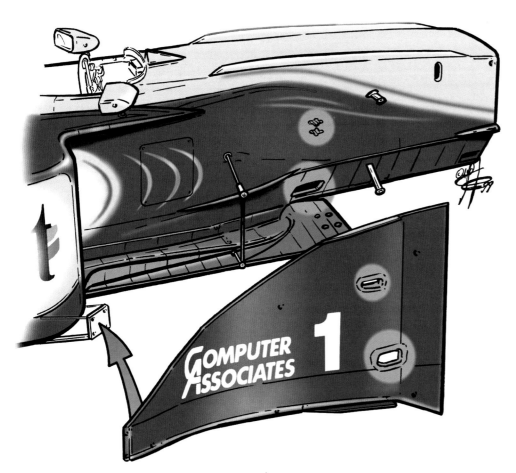

laborious. With regards to the front suspension, both McLaren and Ferrari in effect retained the horizontal torsion bar layouts introduced in '98 and illustrated in the «Suspension» chapter (see page 43). Working on the MP4/14 was more laborious, especially the replacement of the anti-roll bar and the adjustment of ride-height, and in general all operations proved to take longer compared with the same work on the F399. The prize for the most complex procedure went to the replacement of the large barge-boards behind the McLaren's front wheels. On the Ferrari and the other cars this task required just a few minutes while the McLaren mechanics would take around an hour. Newey designed the barge-boards as one-piece elements with holes (highlighted in orange) for the passage of the suspension so as not to reduce torsional stiffness. In order to remove the barge-boards, the suspension arms and accessory elements such as wheel retention cables, electronic cabling, brake calipers and the relative hydraulic circuits all had to be disconnected. Once the barge-boards had been taken off and the procedure repeated in reverse, the suspension set-up had to be checked and the hydraulic circuit for the brakes had to be bled. This operation had to be performed during qualifying for the GP of Europe because Coulthard had damaged his right-hand barge-board. The mechanics sawed straight through both elements and on that occasion mounted those usually used for private testing (bottom) that feature two small removable sections that avoid having to dismantle the suspension. This short-cut undoubtedly irritated the perfectionist Newey but in the end allowed a time saving of around 60%.

## McLAREN - BARGE-BOARDS

This chapter concentrates on the maintenance and set-up procedures effected by the mechanics of the two teams that contested the championship title. Once again, the characteristics of the two rivals emerge, with the more sophisticated MP4/14 reflecting Newey's refusal to accept any compromise in

his search for maximum performance. This resulted in the Anglo-German car suffering from numerous teething troubles early in the season and, above all, proving to be more difficult to set up and more complicated to work on. The general layout of the car was unchanged from the MP4/13 albeit with two important innovations regarding the work of the mechanics with the introduction for the first time of torsion bars in the rear suspension, a feature that actually simplified rear-end adjustments, and the new central location of the oil reservoir which instead made the replacement of the engine trickier and more

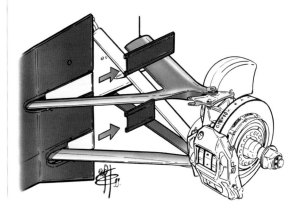

## FERRARI - TORSION BARS

Ferrari once again proved to be the easier car to work on in terms of adjustments in the pits, despite the introduction of a brand-new and sophisticated rear suspension system with horizontal torsion bars concealed within the upper part of the carbonfibre gearbox spacer. The front-end remained unchanged with respects to the F300 of '98, the easy replacement of the torsion bars on which is illustrated above. The other procedures were identical, with the ride-height easily adjusted via the two small holes in the upper part of the chassis. This feature was effectively adopted at the rear too and is highlighted in the two drawings illustrating the sequence followed in replacing the torsion bars. These were mounted with a slight inclination to facilitate their replacement (1). (2) Ride height was adjusted by means of a simple screwdriver as at the front. A clockwise rotation raised the car, the same being true for the increasing or diminishing the incidence of the wings. A clockwise rotation increased the loading. The replacement or disconnection (in the case of rain) of the short anti-roll bar (3) was also easy, as was the adjustment of the third damper (4) linked to the two rockers as at the front.

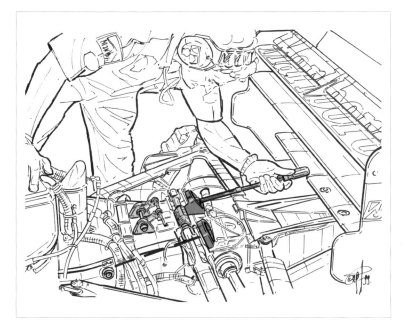

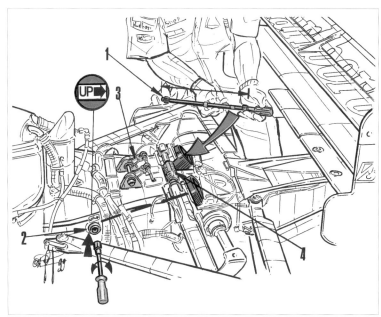

## ELETTRONICALLY CONTROLLED POWER STEERING

The F399's front suspension layout was a direct evolution of that introduced on the F300 in '98 and then copied by almost all the other teams. Visible at the top are the two torsion bars mounted horizontally and easily extractable as shown in the drawing of the F300, top. The vertical dampers were more steeply inclined (4), while the steering column (1), offset to the left, passed between the two pedals to facilitate the use of the large brake pedal with the left foot alone. The only significant change was the electronically controlled power steering jealously concealed during work in the pits. The sensor (2) seen here transmits the steering angle to the CPU controlling the servo-assistance (3) that was generally covered and mounted low on the front bulkhead. In order to provide greater comfort for the drivers, two niches were created in the lower part of the survival cell allowing them to lower the position of their feet, if only by a few centimetres.

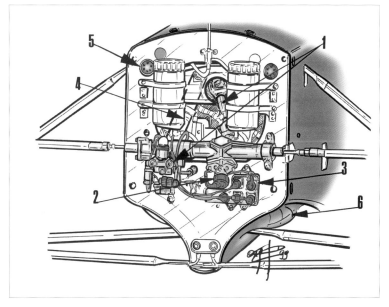

# The two rivals COMPARED

*Ferrari F399*

Just as they had been the previous season, Ferrari and McLaren were again the protagonists in the '99 championship with the F 399 and the MP4/14 contesting the two titles up to the last race. The Constructors' Championship went to Maranello for the first time since way back in 1983, while Ron Dennis' team took the drivers' title after a long struggle with Eddie Irvine who assumed the mantle of number one driver after the dramat-

ic accident at Silverstone that kept Michael Schumacher away from the tracks for no less than 6 GPs. In many ways the two cars displayed contrasting design approaches, starting with the design of their noses, high for the F399, low for the MP4/14, and continuing with the size of barge-boards behind the front wheels and the shape of the side-pods. The engineering philosophies were also different with Ferrari proving to be a less extreme evo-

*McLaren MP4/14*

lution of the '98 car and thus very reliable and easier to drive and set-up. The more highly evolved McLaren on the other hand paid dearly for its excessive search for outright performance with greater mechanical fragility and more critical handling that was trickier to govern at the limit. Adrian Newey even had to go back to certain features from the previous season such as the low steering link mountand different suspension geometry in order to recover some the car's lost driveability, whilst Ross Brawn ordered the modification of the end sections of the side-pods in front of the rear wheels which were aerodynamically less efficient than those of McLaren's Italian rival. The two drawings represent the cars as they lined up for the Japanese GP that spilt the two titles: the drivers' championship going to Hakkinen and McLaren, the constructors' to Ferrari.

# FERRARI

throughout the season, while there was a return to the 1970s (see the Downforce chapter, page 48) with a similar feature also being adopted at the rear for the ultra-fast tracks of Hockenheim and Monza. The congenital problem of aerodynamic interference in the area in front of the rear wheels unfortunately remained, despite the introduction of flip ups very similar to those adopted by McLaren in '98. A new feature was introduced for the French GP, this time inspired by the contemporary McLaren MP4/15, with the elimination of the hot air from the upper part of the side-pods. This last feature was used in almost all the subsequent GPs with the exception of those at Hockenheim and Monza where at speeds over 300 kmh it created undesirable lift at the rear of the car. The engine evolutions were extremely well planned and effective: the 048B debuted in qualifying in Canada and was first raced at the British GP, while the C version was introduced for qualifying at the GP of Europe and raced in Malesia where Ferrari scored its third one-two victory of the season thanks to a masterly performance from Schumacher on his return to racing after the accident at Silverstone.

### ENGINE AIR INTAKE
Great attention was paid to the aerodynamics at the rear of the cockpit in order to improve the efficiency of the engine air intake and the air flow to the rear wing.

Ferrari finally conquered its first world championship title since 1983 and the C3, thanks to reliability and consistency that were decisively superior to those of its chief rival the McLaren MP4/14. The F399 was a logical development of the car that in '98 had challenged for both the drivers' and constructors' championship, but had lost both at the last race of the season. The '99 car proved its worth by completing race after race with no mechanical problems (only one retirement due to a technical failure), covering 93% of the total number of laps comprising the F1 season, a remarkable record given what happened to Schumacher at the first corner of the British GP. The car that permitted the team to achieve such an important goal was derived from the '98 car of which it retained the basic specification such as the increased wheelbase (com-

pared with the original F300 design), the shape and ground clearance of the nose and the layout of the mechanical organs and the front suspension. The rear suspension was instead highly innovative with a layout inspired by the one introduced at the front in 1998 and equipped with horizontal torsion bars and vertical dampers either side of the gearbox. The drawing highlights the differences (detached) with respects to the '98 car. The position of the main body of the car in relation to the two axles was modified. In practice, the driver and the side-pods were set further back with respects to the front axle in order to improve aerodynamic efficiency, with the weight distribution easily modified thanks to the considerable ballast carried — upwards of 50 kg. Great attention was paid to the cockpit area which was modified front and rear with the base

of the engine air intake being notably tapered. The exhausts blowing from the upper surface of the body introduced on the F 300 at the Spanish GP in '98 were retained. The F399 also used delta-shape front wings

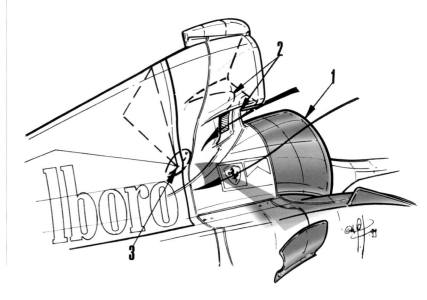

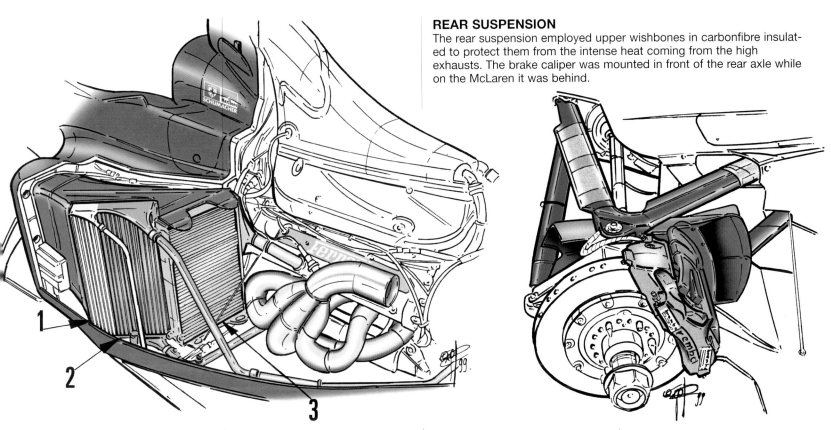

## REAR SUSPENSION

The rear suspension employed upper wishbones in carbonfibre insulated to protect them from the intense heat coming from the high exhausts. The brake caliper was mounted in front of the rear axle while on the McLaren it was behind.

1) The headrest was very long and rounded, with a separation of the air flow between the upper part (2) and the lower section that narrows to such an extent that fake protection structures were required (detached in the drawing, right) so as to respect the minimum dimensions specified in the regulations (3). These «ears» were not fitted at the presentation of the car, only appearing in Australia.

## RADIATORS

The F399 used a very different radiator layout compared with the one used by McLaren with simple fan-like elements. On the Ferrari the water radiators (one each side) were transverse (3), whilst the oil coolers were set in fan formations and separated in two areas: highlighted in yellow the one for gearbox (1) and in green that of the engine. The F399 used high exhausts throughout the season.

## GEARBOX

The layout of the gearbox-spacer assembly was unchanged with respects to the F300 with the gearbox casing (1) in fabricated titanium and the spacer in carbonfibre. The deformable structure acting as the support for the rear wing with the rear suspension mounts was different (3).

The spacer carrying the suspension rocker (4) and the housings for the torsion bars was also new. 2) Differential casing. 5) Small additional supports to prevent the engine cover flexing at high speed. 6) Ride height adjuster. 7) Oil reservoir filler-cap. 8) Wishbone mounts. 9) Engine coupling pins.

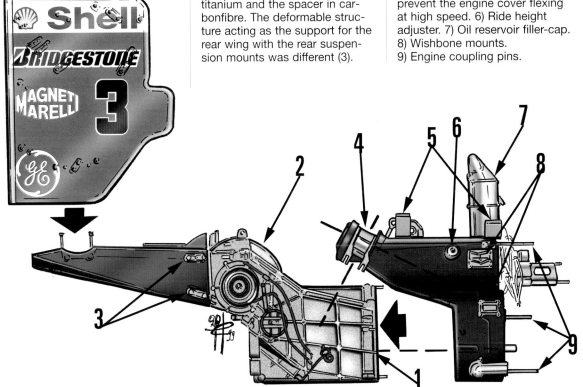

69

## EVOLUTION OF THE COKE BOTTLE AREA

Ferrari made a series of modifications to the so-called Coke-bottle area and the fins in front of the rear wheels. Brazil saw the debut of a version equipped with a small Gurney flap and a lower fairing (first drawing, right) to prevent the hot air from the radiators hitting the rear tyres (see dotted line), accelerating their deterioration, as happened with the original version. On the basis of the modifications introduced in Brazil, in Canada enormous vents (2) were opened in the upper central section of the engine cover with the radiators visible through the apertures. The McLaren-style hot air vent (1) debuted in France (on the left, a comparison with the old version), with the addition of a small flap (2) and a vertical plate (3). In the lower section there was a second air vent (4) with the Coke-bottle area extended (5). A variation with the vents elongated (1) forwards and conspicuously cut away on the inside made their debuts in qualifying in Hungary and were raced in Malesia.

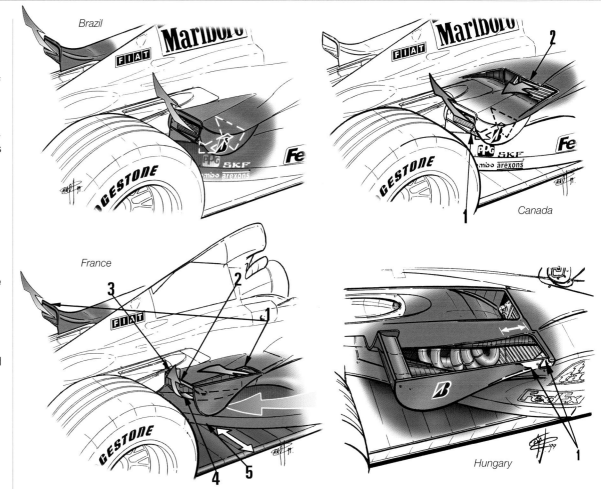

Brazil

Canada

France

Hungary

## BALLAST

The F399 was significantly underweight; at least 50 kg below the minimum thus allowing ballast to be used to adjust the trim according to the track conditions. The drawing illustrates the two different kinds of ballast: slim plates (visible almost in the centre of the car) prohibited after the Spanish GP and tungsten discs which like the titanium plaques had an area of 20 cm².

## SENSORS

Brazil saw a return of the tyre temperature sensors. The one at the front was mounted inside the end-plate (1). Note the single vertical fin (2) of the front wing, combined with a curvature of the horizontal part of the external plate.

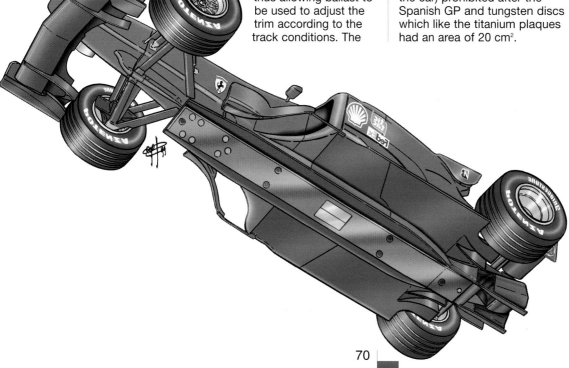

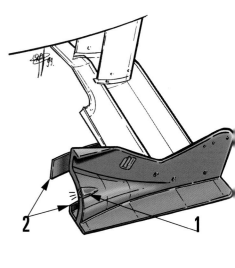

## SAN MARINO

A new front wing with end-plates equipped with a conspicuous fin (1) in place of the small tab on the version introduced in '98 made its debut at Imola. Above all, this wing gave origin to a new family of front wing profiles, all delta-shapes but featuring reduced chords and a new profile (2) that was to be retained in various forms at many other circuits.

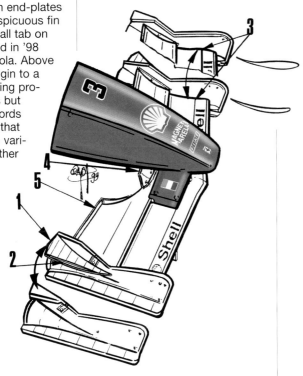

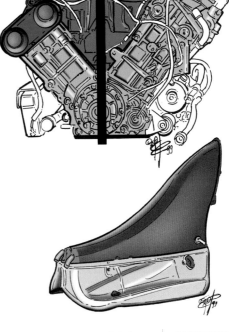

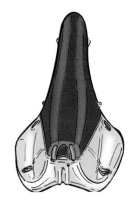

## CANADA

The Montreal track is particularly hard on brakes and a new cooling air intake was introduced. The very long, square-cut intake drew air from the lower part of the front wing, in contrast with the McLaren system.

## ENGINE

During the season two evolutions of the engine were presented. The last version, the 048C, was characterised by a significantly more compact cylinder head which, thanks to a new valve-gear layout (see the comparison drawing with the earlier version), resulted in a useful lowering of the centre of gravity. The block, including the location of the ancillaries such as the alternator,

was unchanged (bottom right). During the year various types of air box were used, inspired by those introduced by Renault in '98 and also used by Sauber.

## SCHUMACHER'S CRASH

Schumacher's dramatic accident on the first lap of the British GP was caused by a loss of pressure in the rear circuit due to a bleed nipple (highlighted in yellow) loosened by vibration.

## AUSTRIAN GP

At the successive Austrian GP the Ferraris presented a single minor modification to the brake caliper lock-nut which was equipped with minute split pins bonded to the caliper with mastic (in orange), on the start-line.

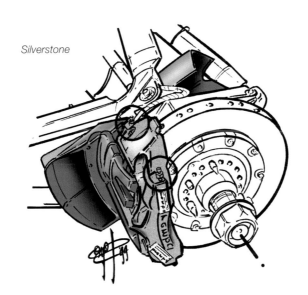

*Silverstone*

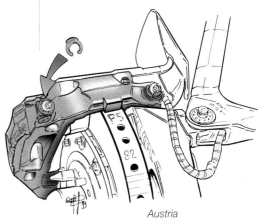

*Austria*

*Australia*

*Brazil*

*Canada*

## ENGINE COVERS

The F399 was fitted with 7 different types of engine cover selected on the basis of the ambient temperature and the type of circuit. The first cover was used in Australia only, while for the successive race in Brazil the hot air venting was modified to prevent the rear tyres «cooking». A small gurney flap was added together with a horizontal plane in the lower part of the fin. This basic engine cover was then used up to the French GP and subsequently only at Hockenheim and Monza. At the Canadian GP huge air vents were opened in the upper section. A new McLaren-style version debuted in France with the flaps and the hot air vent in the upper part. Successively two different type of additional vent were used in the races, single on the left-hand side in Austria and Belgium, and double in Hungary. In Malesia a version with elongated vents and cut away internal walls made its debut in the race.

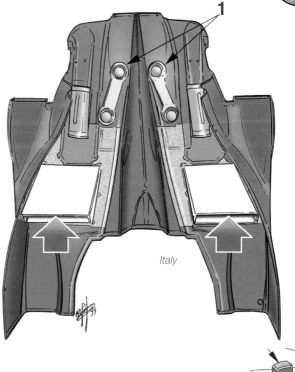

*Italy*

*Malaysia*

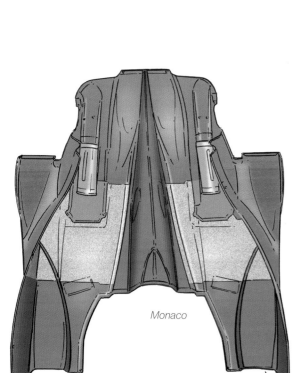

*Monaco*

## ENGINE COVERS SEEN FROM BELOW

The observation of the engine covers from below allows us to note the addition of tabs to prevent damaging flexion at high speed from the German GP onwards. These tabs were first attached to the upper part of the gearbox (1) visible in the drawing left/right/above/below. The two covers also differ in the large hot air vents opened for the Italian GP at Monza. The drawing of the suspension shows the heavily inclined position of the dampers (2) and the third bump stop element (3) between the two rockers.

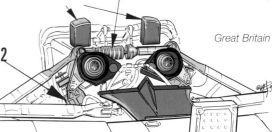

*Great Britain*

France

Hungary

Austria

## AERODYNAMIC PACKAGE FOR FAST CIRCUITS

This series of drawings illustrates the aerodynamic package used at Hockenheim and Monza only. The front wing had a main plane with a reduced chord (1) combined with a flap with a very narrow chord (2), doubled intermediate vanes (2) with the central element being very high (3) and the external one lacking a fin (5). The lateral channels of the diffuser were modified as highlighted in both drawings. In the rear view, note how the horizontal knife-edge part is raised, mirroring the feature introduced by Williams in San Marino. The package also included the delta-shaped rear wing. The drawing shows the Monza version with a flap added to the lower section and a new rear light position (see the Downforce chapter, page 50).

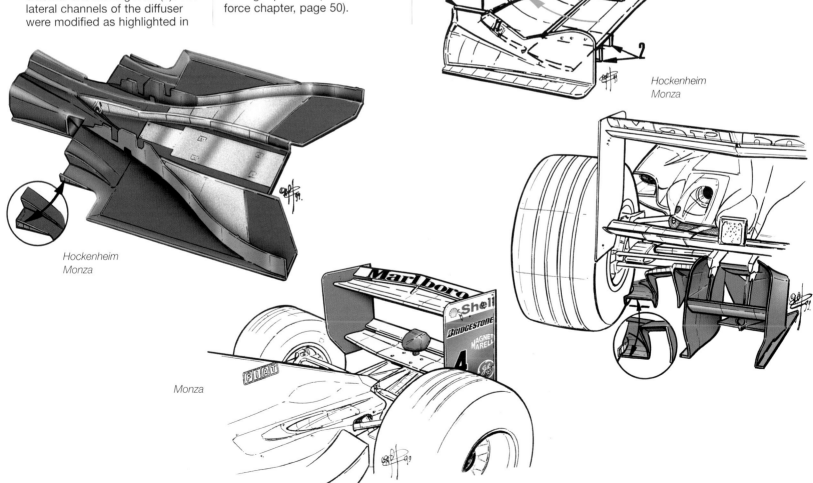

Hockenheim
Monza

Hockenheim
Monza

Monza

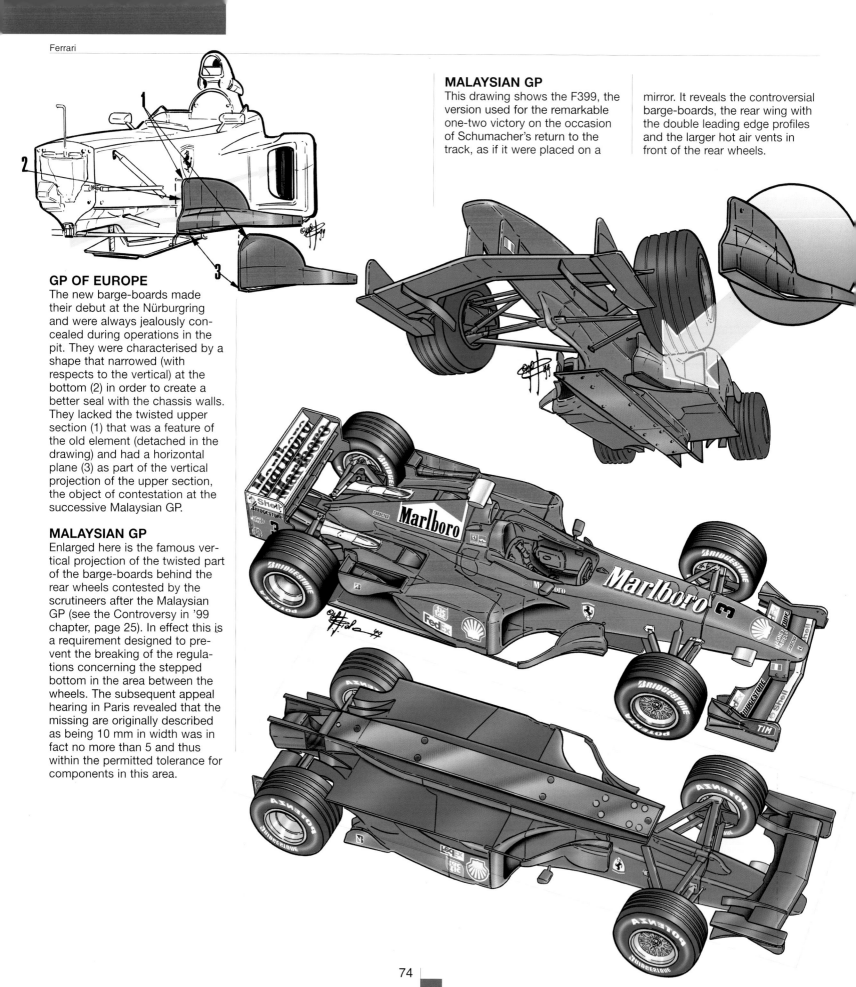

## MALAYSIAN GP
This drawing shows the F399, the version used for the remarkable one-two victory on the occasion of Schumacher's return to the track, as if it were placed on a mirror. It reveals the controversial barge-boards, the rear wing with the double leading edge profiles and the larger hot air vents in front of the rear wheels.

## GP OF EUROPE
The new barge-boards made their debut at the Nürburgring and were always jealously concealed during operations in the pit. They were characterised by a shape that narrowed (with respects to the vertical) at the bottom (2) in order to create a better seal with the chassis walls. They lacked the twisted upper section (1) that was a feature of the old element (detached in the drawing) and had a horizontal plane (3) as part of the vertical projection of the upper section, the object of contestation at the successive Malaysian GP.

## MALAYSIAN GP
Enlarged here is the famous vertical projection of the twisted part of the barge-boards behind the rear wheels contested by the scrutineers after the Malaysian GP (see the Controversy in '99 chapter, page 25). In effect this is a requirement designed to prevent the breaking of the regulations concerning the stepped bottom in the area between the wheels. The subsequent appeal hearing in Paris revealed that the missing are originally described as being 10 mm in width was in fact no more than 5 and thus within the permitted tolerance for components in this area.

## SEQUENCE OF CARS

The sequence of illustrations on these pages is intended to provide a rapid overview of the modifications introduced during the '99 season which culminated in the conquest of the Constructors' Championship at the last race.

## BRAZILIAN GP

New barge-boards behind the wheels, modified area in front of rear wheels, hot air vents (for the race) in the engine cover and tyre temperature sensors.

## SAN MARINO GP

Front wing again delta-shaped but all new.

## SPANISH GP

Brazil-style configuration with supplementary vents in the engine cover.

## AUSTRALIAN GP

Compared with the presentation, at the first race of the season «ears» had been added to the engine air intake and the wings seen in '98 were fitted.

## MONACO GP

First high downforce track with new wings front and rear. Suspension reinforced, greater steering angles.

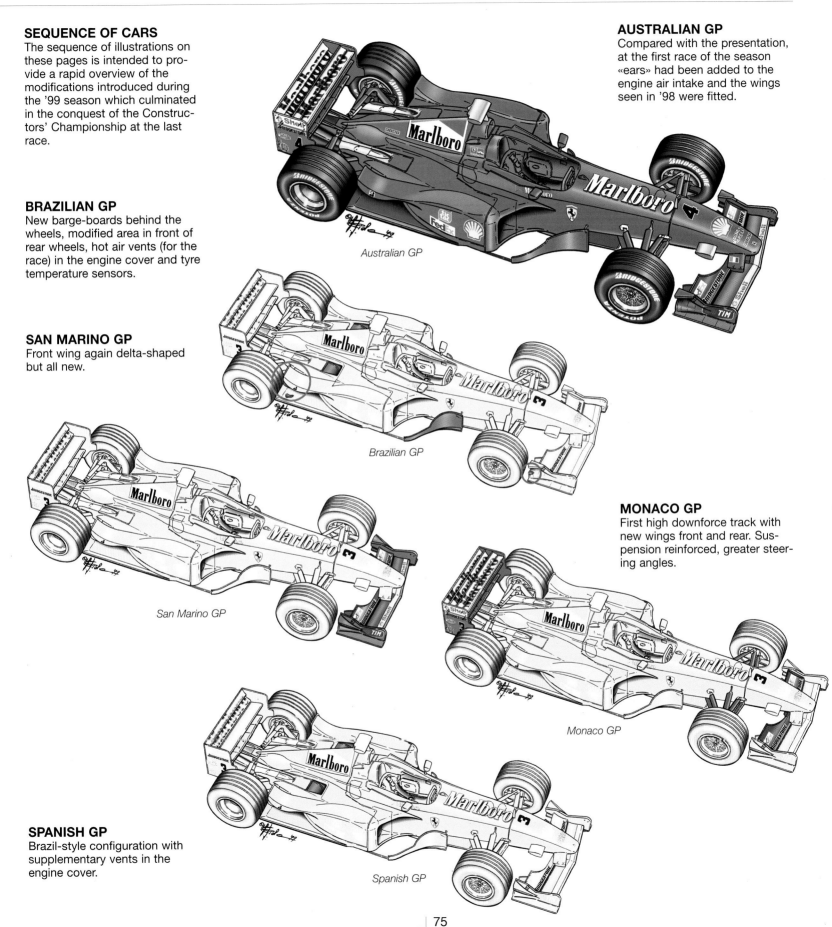

*Australian GP*

*Brazilian GP*

*San Marino GP*

*Monaco GP*

*Spanish GP*

### CANADIAN GP
New front brake air intakes used at Montreal only, qualifying debut of 048B engine, enormous air vents opened for the race.

### FRENCH GP
New McLaren-style Coke-bottle area with vents in upper section. Different front suspension upper wishbone mount.

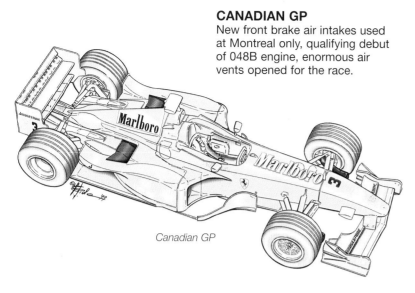

*Canadian GP*

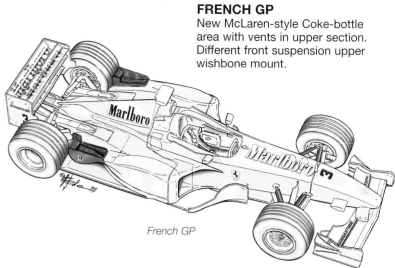

*French GP*

### BRITISH GP
Race debut of the 048B and reinforcements applied to the engine cover. Asymmetric air vents.

### AUSTRIAN GP
After Schumacher's accident at Silverstone the only modification concerned the fixing of the brake caliper bleed nipple.

*British GP*

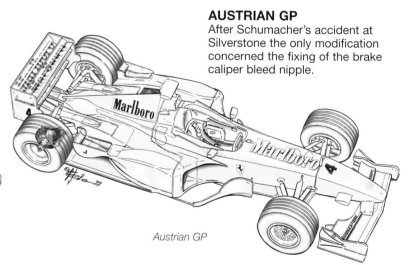

*Austrian GP*

### GERMAN GP
New aerodynamic package for ultra-fast tracks comprising a new delta rear wing and a new diffuser profile combined with a front wing featuring a very narrow chord. Return to old-style bodywork.

### HUNGARIAN GP
Monaco-type wings combined with new bodywork with larger hot air vents.

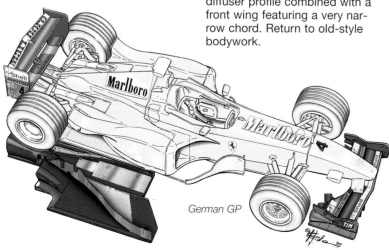

*German GP*

*Hungarian GP*

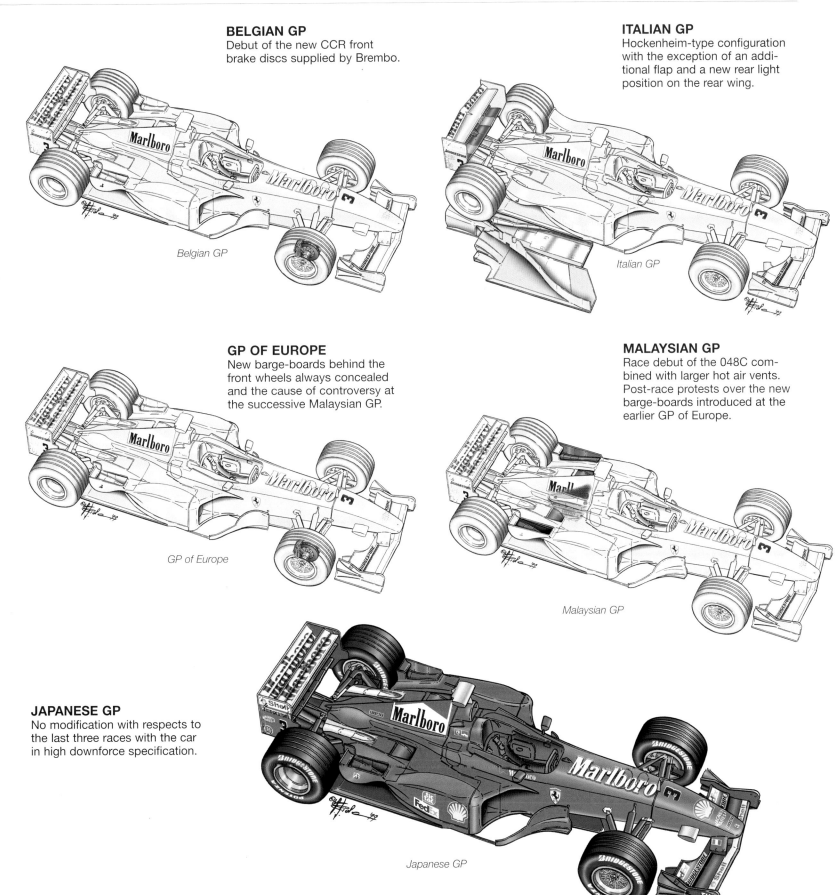

**BELGIAN GP**
Debut of the new CCR front
brake discs supplied by Brembo.

*Belgian GP*

**ITALIAN GP**
Hockenheim-type configuration
with the exception of an additional flap and a new rear light
position on the rear wing.

*Italian GP*

**GP OF EUROPE**
New barge-boards behind the
front wheels always concealed
and the cause of controversy at
the successive Malaysian GP.

*GP of Europe*

**MALAYSIAN GP**
Race debut of the 048C combined with larger hot air vents.
Post-race protests over the new
barge-boards introduced at the
earlier GP of Europe.

*Malaysian GP*

**JAPANESE GP**
No modification with respects to
the last three races with the car
in high downforce specification.

*Japanese GP*

# McLAREN

Mika Hakkinen had to work hard for his second World Championship title: he had to cope with both internal rivalry with his team-mate David Coulthard and the technical characteristics of the new MP4/14 that, from the first race of the season, proved to be highly competitive but difficult to drive and set up and less reliable than the earlier MP4/13. The second car designed for McLaren by the genial Adrian Newey reflected his well known refusal to accept compromises, a virtue that is at times upheld at the expense of the car as a whole. From its presentation on the eve of the new season, the MP4/14 was clearly a more highly evolved design than its predecessor. There were innovations in almost all areas, from the wheelbase and weight distribution values through to the aerodynamic package and the suspension layout. After having established a standard with the introduction of a long wheelbase car, McLaren reduced this parameter on the MP4/14, with the

weight distribution slightly favouring the rear axle. Compared with the '98 car, the detail changes were as follows: the wheelbase was around 3 cm shorter, with the position of the front axle with respects to the survival cell slightly different, the chassis extending further forwards. This led to a gain in terms of the section of the channels inboard of the wheels, with significantly improved air flow quality towards the side-pods which were set further back, as was the cockpit and driver by at least 10-15 cm. While respecting the restrictions imposed by the FIA, the chassis dimensions at the front were further reduced, with both the upper and lower parts of the false structural fins increased in size compared with those introduced on the '98 car. In order to improve front-end aerodynamics, the nose was

longer, thus ensuring a more efficient front wing. The shape of the side-pods was very different, both at the entrance and in the critical area in front of the rear wheels where the vanes introduced in '98 and copied by Ferrari were replaced by a more sophisticated design. Hot air was extracted in the upper part before the vanes, in front of the wheels which were shielded by conspicuous vertical fairings. The size and shape of the large barge-boards behind the front wheels were virtually unchanged, as was the diffuser. Two of Adrian Newey's objectives with the MP4/14 design were the lowering of the centre of gravity and weight and the concentration of mass around the centre of gravity. Hence the decision to shift the oil reservoir from the classic

location between the engine and gearbox to within the fuel tank, with a notable rationalisation of the cooling system pipework. The drastic reduction in weight allowed the team to juggle with around 70 kg of ballast when fine-tuning weight distribution according to the demands of the various circuits. After having introduced steering arms attached to the middle of the uprights in '98 (first drawing, top, on the facing page), the MP4/14 surprisingly returned to steering arms attached at the top together with the upper wishbone (centre), a layout abandoned at the Austrian GP in favour of the '98 set-up to allow different front suspension geometries (bottom drawing). There was another new

**'98**

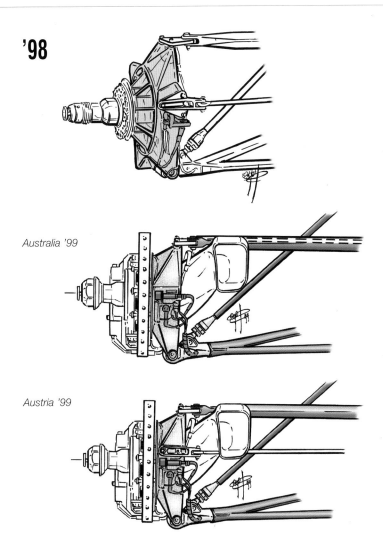

*Australia '99*

*Austria '99*

centre of gravity. There was a notable tapering in the so-called Coke-bottle area, with increased air flow over the lower bodywork.

The use of part of the hot air from the radiators to accelerate the air flow directed towards the rear wing was a new feature.

feature at the rear where the McLaren was fitted with torsion bars in place of classic coil springs. Mario Illien's engine contributed to the reduction in weight but required the design of a new 7-speed gearbox to overcome the torque deficit. The new Mercedes 10-cylinder unit also suffered from increased vibration and a higher working temperature which gave rise to reliability problems early in the season. Teething troubles convinced the powers-that-be at McLaren to launch a development programme that, however, did not always result in definitive modifications used in the GPs (see the high exhausts and the extended wheelbase tested in two private sessions, and the different rear suspension layout tested in the second half of the season but never raced).

**TOP VIEW**

The comparison from above between the old MP4/13 (left) and the new MP4/14 (right) shows how the air passage at the front was enlarged thanks to the slightly set-back front bulkhead affected by the 30 cm minimum width rule. Early in the season, in order to further privilege aerodynamics, the steering arms were faired within the upper wishbone. The setting back of the driver and the shortening of the side-pods provided greater aerodynamic efficiency at the centre and front of the car. The front wheels were, in fact, further away from the side-pods. At the rear the chassis contained both the oil reservoir and the fuel tank and extended the full 80 cm in width permitted by the regulations. In this way much of the mass is concentrated around the

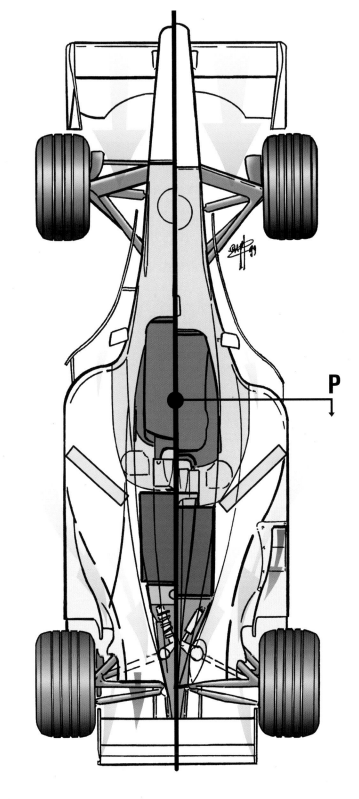

P

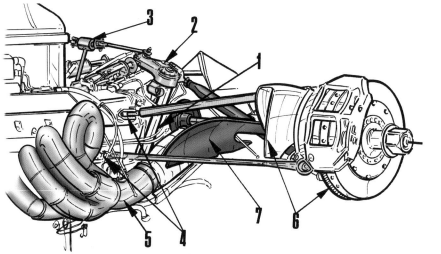

## OIL RESERVOIR

Adrian Newey would have liked to introduce the central oil reservoir location on the '98 car but opted instead for the tried and trusted position between engine and gearbox. On the MP4/14 he followed the lead of Stewart, Arrows and Prost, adopting a feature that allowed mass to be concentrated around the centre of gravity and considerable weight savings. The plumbing was in fact shorter and it was less complicated to replace the engine which could be detached without disturbing the cooling system.

## REAR SUSPENSION

The adoption of torsion bars in the rear suspension (introduced by Barnard in '89) was a new direction for McLaren. Newey created a layout inspired by that of Barnard's '98 Arrows, with external torsion bars (1) visible either side of the gearbox. The rocker (2) was again very long and carried linkages to the anti-roll bar (3) pivoting on the centre of the gearbox. The wishbone mounts (4) were very close together and offered two different anti-squat settings. The exhausts (5) initially merged into a single large terminal which then bifurcated. 6) Large front brake disc cooling duct. 7) The suspension had to be dismantled to remove this bodywork element.

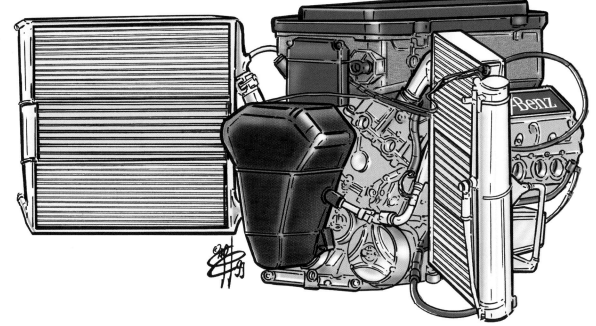

## AIRFLOW

Like the previous year's car, the MP4/14 featured a low nose with no negative effects on the quality of air flow over the car. The front wing exploited the maximum permitted width of 140 cm, although the end-plates narrowed in the area in front of the wheels. There was a new flow pattern in the area in front of the rear wheels where the air passage in the lower part (the Coke-bottle area) was increased. Hot air from the radiators was channelled to the upper part in an area shielded to avoid damaging the flow towards the rear wing.

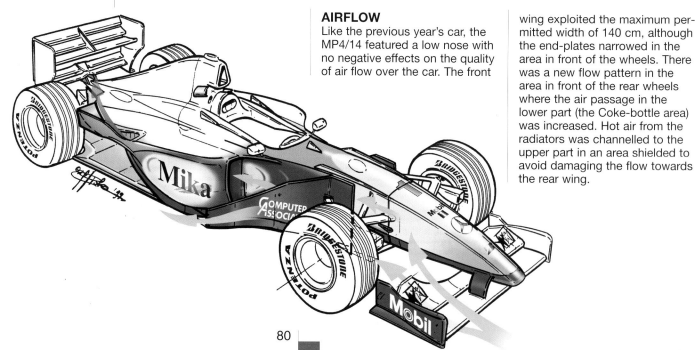

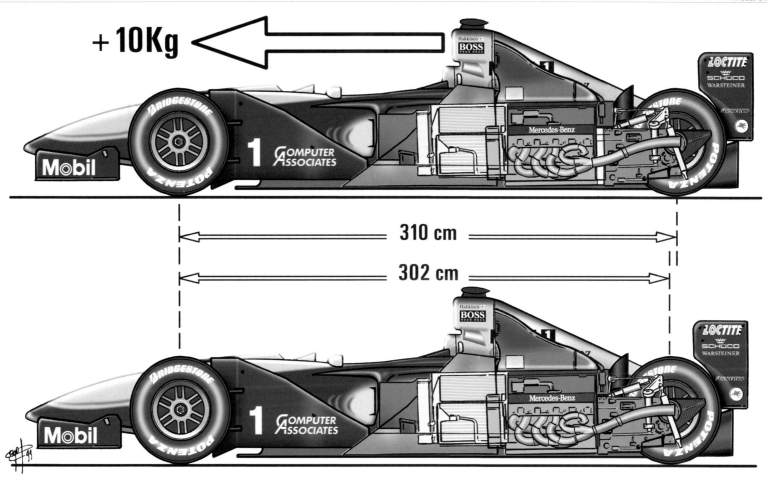

**+10Kg**

310 cm

302 cm

### LONG WHEELBASE

The 1999 McLaren proved to be very edgy and less easy to drive than the previous season's car and following the opening races was thus subjected to a number of experiments including the lengthening of the wheelbase and the fitting of high exhausts. Hakkinen's crash during the San Marino GP, in contrast with the one at the chicane in the Italian GP, was largely due to the difficulty in controlling the car on the kerbs compared with the MP4/13. High exhausts were tested to try to solve the overheating problems suffered in the first two races. The longer wheelbase was obtained via a spacer of around 8 cm between the engine and gearbox. This feature, tested in a private session in late June/early July, was taken no further. In theory it

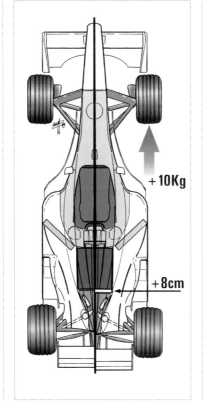

+10Kg

+8cm

allowed a different weight distribution with around 10 kg being shifted to the front axle, the crucial 70 kg of ballast available to McLaren then being used to best effect. The long wheelbase version should have made the car less critical and easier to control. Due to make its debut at the British GP, this version was never actually raced.

### HIGH EXHAUSTS

High exhausts were tested immediately after the Brazilian GP to try to resolve the reliability problems suffered in the first two races. These problems were then overcome without the need for this feature, felt to be counterproductive from the point of view of aerodynamics at the back of the car.

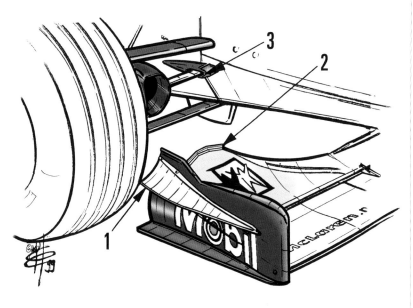

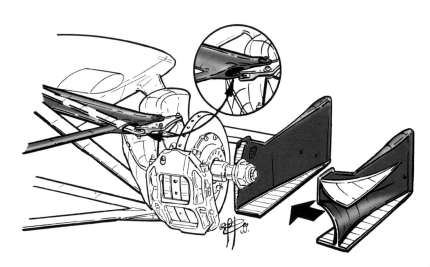

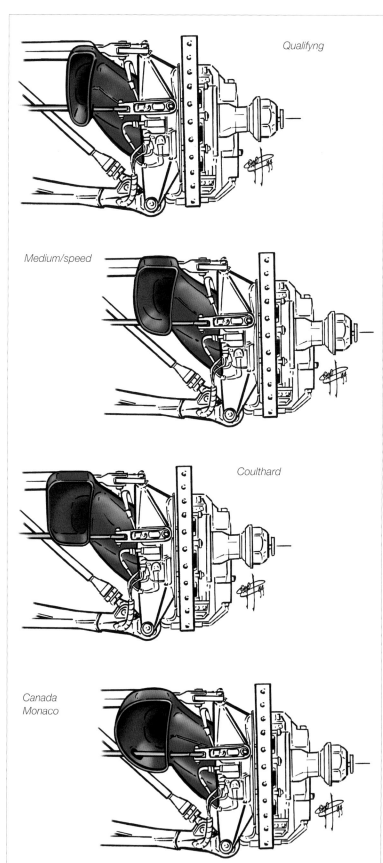

*Qualifyng*

*Medium/speed*

*Coulthard*

*Canada
Monaco*

## AUSTRIAN GP

The first modifications were made at the Canadian GP with the addition of a third damper to the rear suspension, combined with a different diffuser that was retained until the end of the season. At the following French GP the front wing was modified and fitted with new end-plates which were altered again for the Austrian GP. At Zeltweg steering arms identical to those of the MP4/13 were fitted, in the middle of the upright so as to allow for different suspension geometries and avoid the stiffening up of the steering that occurred at Monaco. In the original version, the steering arms were faired within the aerodynamic upper wishbones, causing considerable production and maintenance difficulties. Again in Austria, new front wing end-plates were introduced featuring conspicuous bent fins (1) on the outside. There was also a new flap (2) with a small Gurney flap. The top drawing shows the steering arm attached in the middle of the upright.

## BRAKE AIR INTAKES

Great care was taken over the shape and size of the brake air intakes which draw air from the upper part of the front wing. Hakkinen, easier on brakes than his team-mate, frequently used the less conspicuous form whenever two options were available. At the top can be seen the very fast track or qualifying intake, used by Hakkinen in the race at Suzuka too. The second intake was used for fast tracks with medium brake use, while the third intake was used on tracks that were hard on brakes (or by Coulthard) and the fourth was used at Monaco and in Canada and Hungary. The drawing shows the version used at Budapest, with the steering arm passing through the intake. This feature was made necessary by the lowering of the steering arm (at Monaco and in Canada it was still attached to the top of the upright).

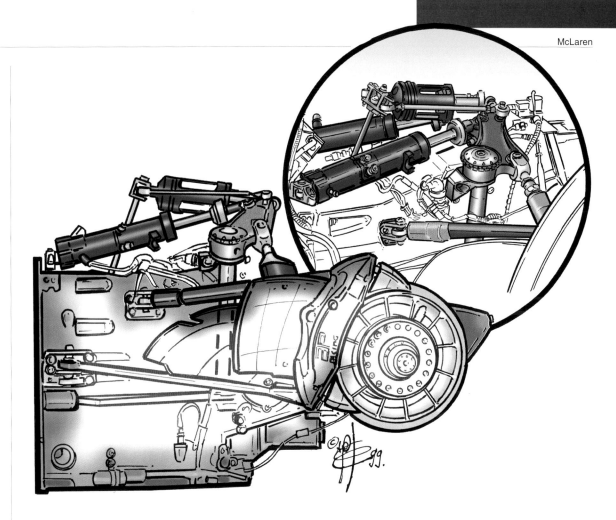

## CANADIAN GP

The '99 Canadian GP saw the debut of the third bump-stop element in the rear suspension. This feature was frequently used in the '98 season but was only adopted on the MP4/14 from the 6th race. The drawing shows the gearbox casting with the mounts (two positions) for the suspension wishbone clearly visible. It was attached to the long suspension rocker and the short anti-roll bar, pivoted at the centre of the gearbox. The brake caliper was attached to the front of the upright so as not to add its weight to the mass cantilevered from the axle.

## DIFFUSER

Again in Canada, a new diffuser was introduced with slightly raised lateral channels (1) and more conspicuous Gurney flaps. Detail modifications were also made to the central channel equipped with a curved plane (2) at the centre of the vertical walls (3) with a large window. Note the presence of a small Gurney flap in the area of the seal with the rear wheels (4).

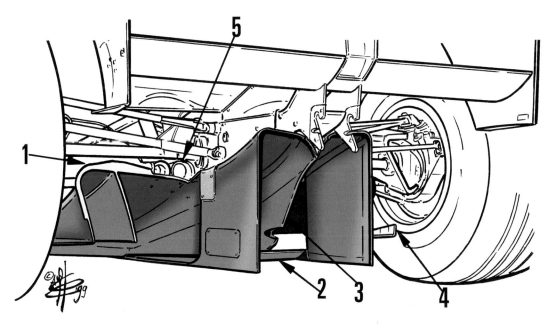

*Standard*

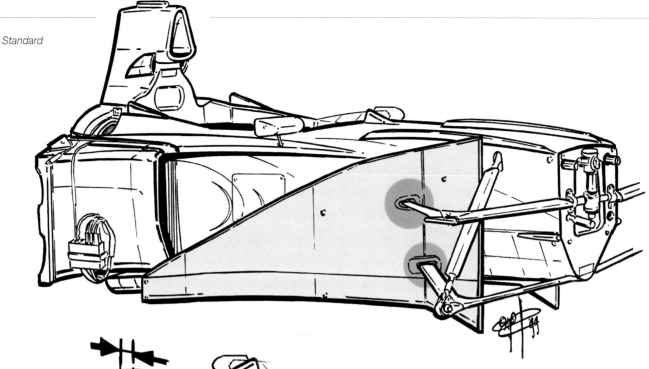

*Japan*

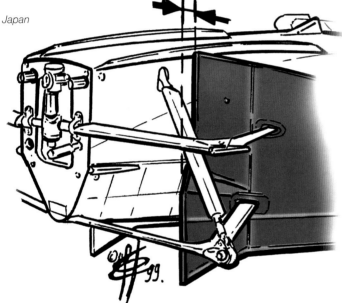

featured a twist that was in some ways similar to that of the highly controversial Ferrari barge-boards. In this case there was no need of the shadow plate because the hollowed-out part was between the wheels and therefore outside the area governed by the vertical projection rule (within the tangents of the wheels).

## BELGIAN GP

Belgium saw the appearance of new lighter rear bodywork elements recognisable by the two small covers in the area above the suspension rockers. This modification was necessary for a new rear suspension layout that was never actually raced but was track-tested at length by the test-driver Heidfield.

## JAPANESE GP

In practice the MP4/14 inherited the large barge-boards behind the front wheels introduced in '98 on the old MP4/13 and composed of an impractical single element with all the inherent problems described on page 64 The holes for the suspension elements are highlighted in colour while at the bottom can be seen how in the area within the central 50 cm, the barge-boards extended 5 cm downwards to a point. New barge-boards were taken to Suzuka  to scrutineering. They were modified at the front and

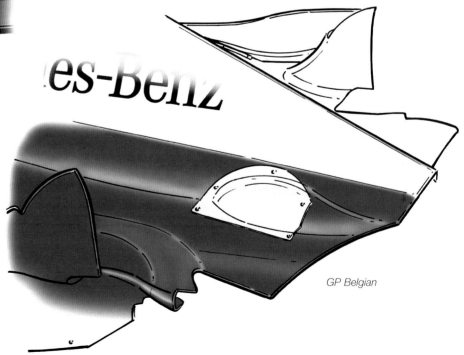

*GP Belgian*

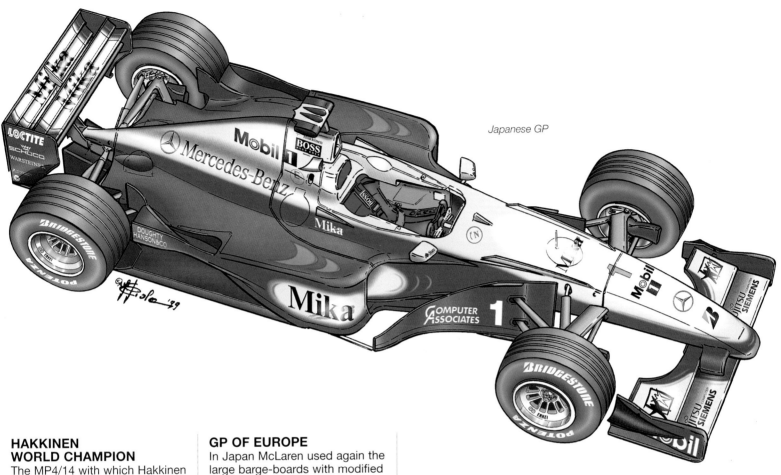

*Japanese GP*

## HAKKINEN WORLD CHAMPION

The MP4/14 with which Hakkinen won the Japanese GP and conquered his second championship title, had a medium-high aerodynamic loading, with the front wing used at the European GP and curved end-plates equipped with external triangular fins. The large barge-boards behind the wheels were fitted with small Gurney flaps at the top, with the relative area of legal shielding introduced at the Nürburgring at the bottom. The barge-boards featuring a inward-curving section similar to the controversial elements used by Ferrari for the last 3 races and tested at Magny Cours before the Japanese GP were instead not used. The rear wing had doubled leading-edge profiles. Both during qualifying and in the race Hakkinen used slimmer brake cooling intakes than those fitted to Coulthard's car. The fourth spare car was not fitted with the lighter engine cover because it was damaged by the Scotsman during qualifying on the Friday.

## GP OF EUROPE

In Japan McLaren used again the large barge-boards with modified top sections introduced at the GP of Europe. They featured small Gurney flaps to increase downforce. At the bottom can be seen the projection required by the regulations that were at the root of Ferrari's problems in Malaysia.

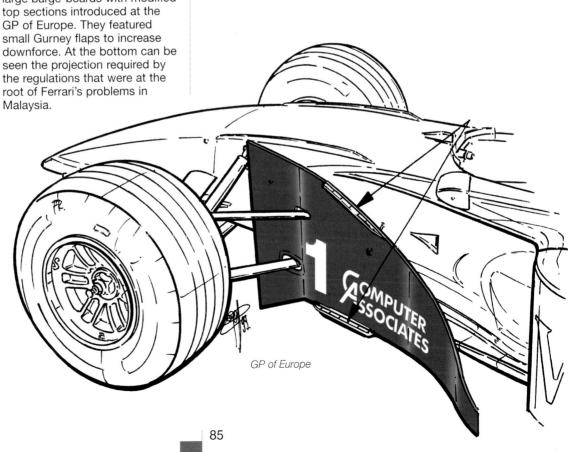

*GP of Europe*

# JORDAN

Having joined the elite group of Grand Prix winning teams in '98 (Hill triumphing in the dramatic Belgian GP), Jordan consolidated this success in the '99 championship with two well deserved victories for Frentzen in the French and Italian GPs. Even more importantly the team finished third in the Constructors' Championship, a notable achievement that rewarded the efforts of one of the youngest outfits in Formula 1 (Jordan having made its debut in '91). The merit lay with an avant-garde car and a Mugen-Honda engine that improved notably during the season. The 199 was the first car produced by Jordan without its original designer Gary Anderson, replaced by Mike Gascoyne (ex-Tyrrell). In various areas, however, it was still influenced by the her-

itage of earlier models such as the general layout of the car and the suspension with coil springs and dampers front and rear. Jordan was also the only car to retain horizontal dampers at the front, located in a cradle in the upper part of the chassis. Gascoyne's hand can be seen in the great care taken over the aerodynamic development of the car and it was no coincidence that this team was the only one to present certain innovations in the field such as the fins in front of the side-pods, the third small winglet behind the roll bar (used

in the Hungarian GP only), and the central section of the car with the fuel tank area so wide and low as to form a single structure with the side-pods. This feature allowed an incredibly small frontal area to be achieved, but aroused a degree of controversy due to the protection structures for the driver's head which were

obligatory according to the regulations but in this case were replaced by two fins that were much higher than those used by all the other teams that raced cars with much taller central fuel tank areas. Jordan was the only team to run, from the very first race, a car with no barge-boards behind the front wheels (subse-

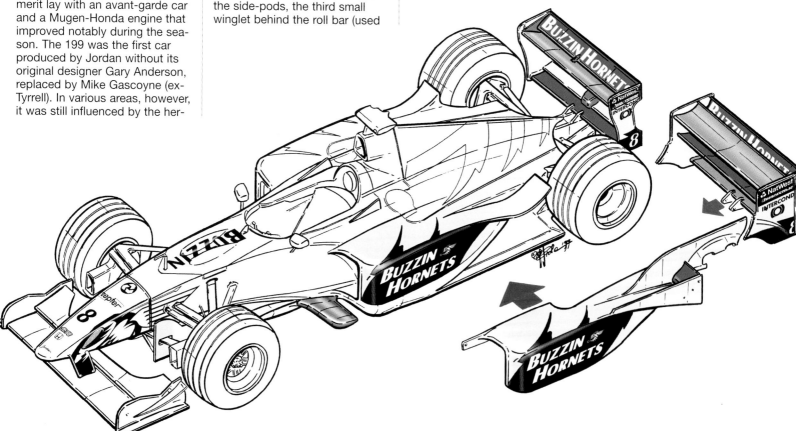

quently imitated by Williams), replaced by elements within the front suspension with the front section inside the central 50 cm zone, and thus 5 cm lower, at the same height as the reference plane, thus creating a better seal with the ground. Jordan was also the only team to systematically alternate two types of rear body-work, made possible thanks to its three-piece structure. The drawing highlights the two extreme versions: Monza (equipped with a brand-new rear wing) with simple, upwards-curving fins in front of the rear wheels, ad the one used for most of the medium-high downforce circuits (detached, with the rear wing fitted at Monaco), characterised by a small flap linked by means of a long extension to the rear wing. Note how the extension and the rear wing end-plate have a conspicuous flare at the bottom to improve the air flow in the delicate area between the rear wheels. Still on the subject of exclusive features, a slight step backwards was made with respects to the engine, no longer fully load-bearing but also attached to the chassis via two conspicuous struts extending from the chassis (see facing page) as on certain cars from the 70s. Jordan also presented two

wheelbase options, although the version lengthened by 64 mm (following pages) was created more to satisfy the preferences of Hill (who exclusively used it from the Austrian GP) than out of real technical necessity.

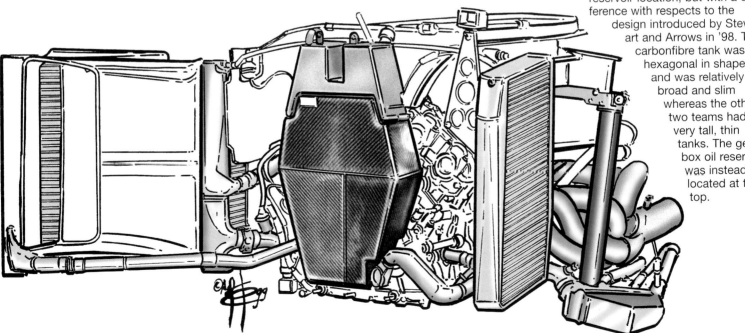

## CHASSIS AND ENGINE MOUNTS

These two drawings highlight the system devised by Mike Gascoyne to ensure greater stiffness of the chassis-engine assembly, countering the continual and extreme lightening of the latest generation power units. At the end of the chassis there were two triangular extensions that locked onto the cylinder heads so as to prevent torsional flexing. In the drawing above of the chassis, it can be seen how the fuel tank area was very low and how the fins either side of the cockpit were effectively the only elements protecting the driver's head.

## OIL RESERVOIR

Jordan adopted the central oil reservoir location, but with a difference with respects to the design introduced by Stewart and Arrows in '98. The carbonfibre tank was hexagonal in shape and was relatively broad and slim whereas the other two teams had very tall, thin tanks. The gearbox oil reservoir was instead located at the top.

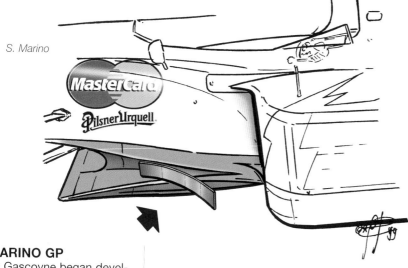

*S. Marino*

## SAN MARINO GP

At Imola Gascoyne began development work on the aerodynamics of the area in front of the side-pods, with a configuration vaguely inspired by that adopted by Benetton for the same area. This small vertical fin was, however, only used in qualifying and was not fitted to the car for the following races, being replaced by the small fairing introduced in Spain.

## SPANISH GP

A modification was introduced at Barcelona that was retained throughout the rest of the season. This was the small wing-shaped fairing that served to improve the quality of the air flow towards the side-pods and the lower part of the car. The feature was to be copied by Williams from the Belgian GP.

*Spain*

## HOCKENHEIM - MONZA

On the ultra-fast tracks of Hockenheim and Monza Jordan introduced a new version of its rear wing, partially reviving a feature seen on the Stewart in '98 with regards the cut-out in the lower section of the end-plates which were also equipped with two small vertical Gurney flaps (in yellow). Clearly, the wing was a biplane design and featured a main-plane at the top with a very reduced chord with respects to that of the flap.

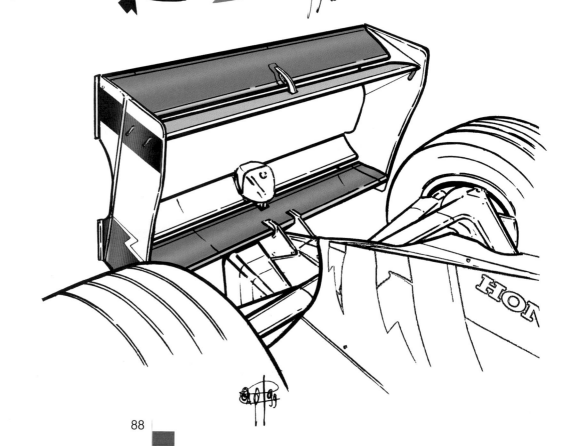

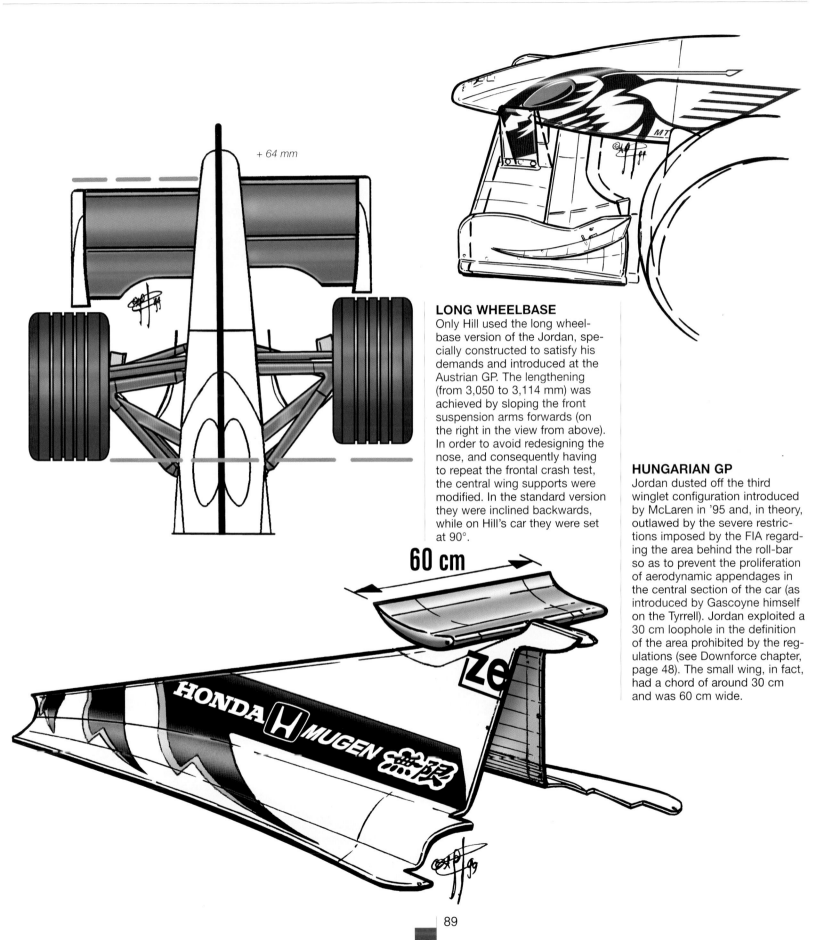

+ 64 mm

## LONG WHEELBASE

Only Hill used the long wheel-base version of the Jordan, specially constructed to satisfy his demands and introduced at the Austrian GP. The lengthening (from 3,050 to 3,114 mm) was achieved by sloping the front suspension arms forwards (on the right in the view from above). In order to avoid redesigning the nose, and consequently having to repeat the frontal crash test, the central wing supports were modified. In the standard version they were inclined backwards, while on Hill's car they were set at 90°.

## HUNGARIAN GP

Jordan dusted off the third winglet configuration introduced by McLaren in '95 and, in theory, outlawed by the severe restrictions imposed by the FIA regarding the area behind the roll-bar so as to prevent the proliferation of aerodynamic appendages in the central section of the car (as introduced by Gascoyne himself on the Tyrrell). Jordan exploited a 30 cm loophole in the definition of the area prohibited by the regulations (see Downforce chapter, page 48). The small wing, in fact, had a chord of around 30 cm and was 60 cm wide.

60 cm

HONDA MUGEN 無限

# STEWART

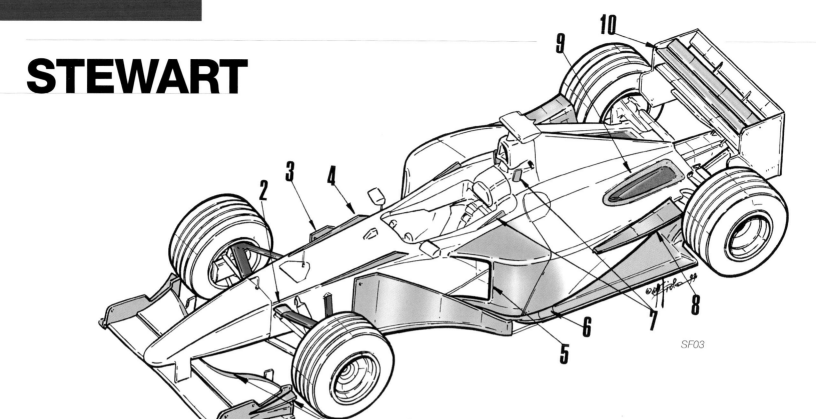

*SF03*

In the '99 season Stewart entered the elite group of teams to have won a Grand Prix, thanks to Johnny Herbert's deserved success in the dramatic GP of Europe. The SF03, conceived by Alan Jenkins before leaving the team and revised and corrected by Gary Anderson who arrived at Stewart in the summer of '98, was the surprise package of the season, leaping from eighth to fourth place in the Constructors' Championship. It was also the car that most closely followed the principles introduced by the McLaren MP4/13 in '98, while still retaining strong ties with the previous year's Stewart. The configuration and shape of the low nose, the survival cell divided into sections with the artifice of the fins in the upper part, the low-set steering arms and the wheelbase dimensions and weight distribution were inspired by Newey's '98 car. Features introduced at the same time on the latest McLaren such as the driver set further back and the distancing of the side-pods from the front axle were also similar. If on the one hand the '99-season Stewart was inspired by the championship-winning '98 McLaren, the latter team instead copied the central oil reservoir location introduced by Jenkins

on the SF02. Stewart abandoned the innovative carbonfibre gearbox casing that had compromised the Scottish team's reliability the previous season when it recorded just 12 finishes from 32 starts. With the new car Stewart immediately positioned itself at the shoulders of Ferrari and McLaren as one of the teams completing the most race laps (78%), and achieved 18 finishes from 32 starts. The number of retirements due to technical problems nonetheless remained fairly high at 12, of which 4 were due to failures of the new 10-cylinder Ford, the field's most innovative engine thanks to the use of new engineering technology and its drastic reduction in size. It was also a somewhat mysterious object as throughout the season nobody managed to

see it despite the desperate attempts of rival engineers and photographers. The radiator packages and the large heat shields protected the unit from prying eyes, as can be seen in the drawing on the following pages.

## COMPARISON SF02-SF03

The two comparison drawings depict the '99 car in the configuration that won the GP of Europe and the old '98 model. The family look was even more apparent in the early season version equipped with side-pod intakes very similar to those of the SF02 (see following pages) and lacking the high exhausts. In '98 the

Stewart already featured a relatively low nose and very large barge-boards behind the front wheels. In '99 the latter resembled those of the McLaren even more closely. 1) The nose of the SF03 derived from that of the earlier car as did the shape of the flaps. The end-plates were instead revised and fitted with external fins. 2) The conspicuous

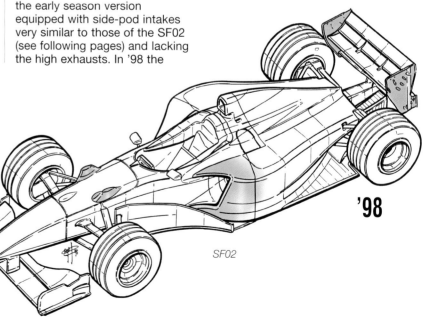

'98

*SF02*

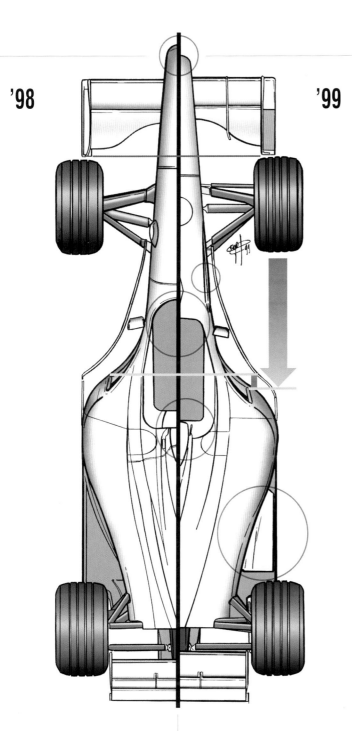

'98    '99

## OVERHEAD VIEW

Comparing the new SF03 (right) with the old SF02 it is interesting to note that almost all the innovations highlighted were also part of the package of modifications introduced by McLaren in '99. This is evidence that the Stewart was more than simply a copy of the previous season's championship-winning car, but rather an optimum interpretation of the concepts expressed by Newey. The chassis was, in fact, set back with respects to the front axle to allow, as on the MP4/14, its width in the area between the wheels to be reduced. The nose was slightly shorter. Again at the same as on Ron Dennis's car, the side-pods were distanced from the front axle to improve the quality of air flow towards the body of the car while the driver was set further back so as alter the weight distribution in favour of the rear axle. The shaping of the Coke-bottle area in front of the rear wheels was different and a semi-horizontal fin was introduced.

## SUSPENSION COMPARISON

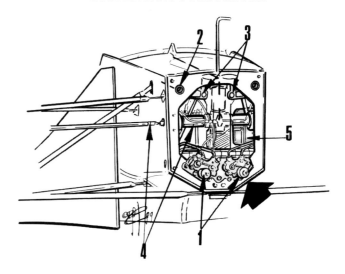

In '98 Ferrari and McLaren introduced a new suspension layout that attracted widespread approval, with Stewart too adopting the system. The torsion bars that on the old SF02 were set vertically (1) with the three horizontal dampers (2) were instead horizontal on the SF03 (2) with the dampers vertical and the rockers (3) concealed within the chassis. The novelty introduced by Jenkins and then modified by Anderson was that of the external location (1) of the dampers' gas cylinders. The steering column and arms (4) were set lower that the upper wishbone. The brake pedal (5) was very large and set well apart from the accelerator.

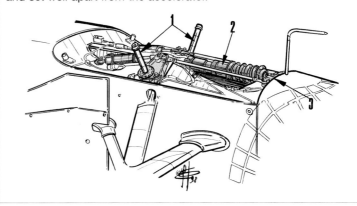

protuberances on the top of the nose were eliminated thanks to a new horizontal torsion bar layout on the SF03 (facing page).
3) The large barge-boards, similar to those of the McLaren were restricted to the height of the suspension uprights. 4) McLaren-like fins were introduced at the top of the chassis to reduce the size of the survival cell.
5) The side-pod intakes, originally similar to those of the SF02, were modified by Anderson for the British GP. 6) The side-pods themselves were slightly narrow-er to allow this small step to be created at the bottom.
7) Either side of the cockpit and the engine air intake there were 4 small fins allowing the dimensions to be reduced while respecting the letter of the regulations. 8) Simple fins were introduced in front of the rear wheels. 9) The high exhausts were adopted from the Belgian GP onwards. 10) The rear wing lost the characteristic end-plates with sculpted lower sections. The drawing shows the GP of Europe wing with high-set forward planes.

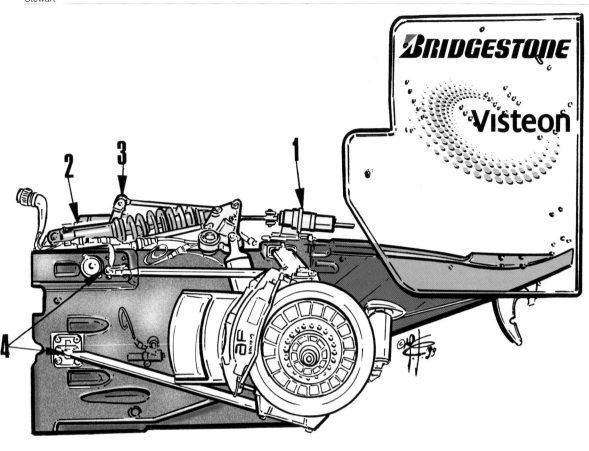

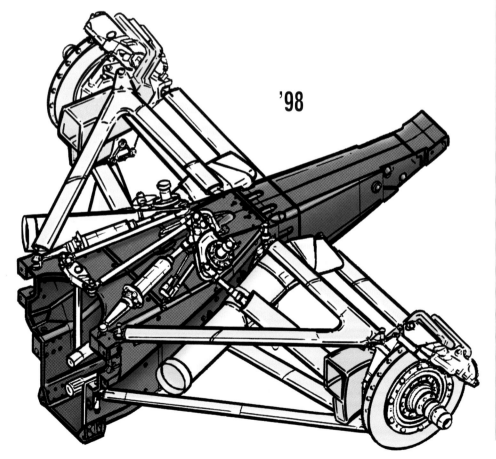

'98

## GEARBOX

The Stewart SF03 lost one of the major innovations introduced the previous year, the carbonfibre gearbox that had been one of the principal causes of the poor reliability that dogged the Scottish cars in '98. The pro-link suspension was instead retained. Despite the cast alloy gearbox casing, the rear-end design was practically unchanged. The drawing also highlights how the rear deformable structure in carbonfibre remained identical to that of the SF02. The rear suspension layout allowed for the use of a third bump-stop element (1) linked by two short rods to the rockers: the anti-roll bar (2) was set forwards, between the two horizontal dampers mounted in a V and also linked (3) to the rockers. The suspension arm mounts (4) were adjustable.

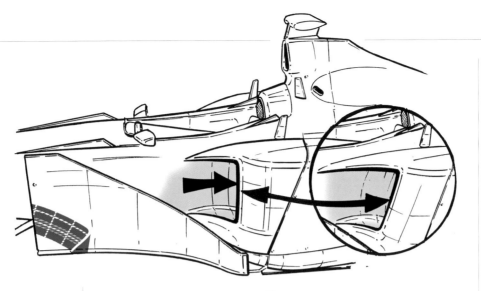

## OIL RESERVOIR

The SF03 retained the central oil reservoir, an innovation introduced in '98 and employed by no less than 8 teams (including Stewart) in '99. The shape of the tank, again made in carbonfibre, remained fairly tall and narrow in contrast with those of other teams such as McLaren, Jordan and Minardi. Note how the large radiator packs (twinned as on the SF02) completely conceal the compact Ford 10-cylinder.

## BRITISH GP

At the British GP Gary Anderson made considerable modifications to the shape of the side-pods, slightly shortening them, but above all abandoning the traditional form of the intake visible in the drawing here. This modification required the repetition of the lateral crash tests as the changes involved the survival cell area.

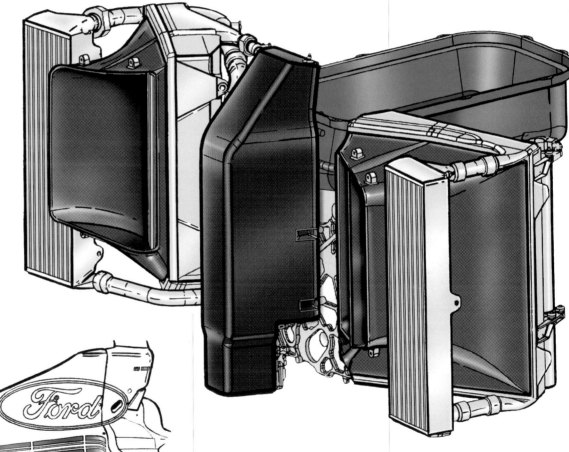

## BELGIAN GP

Stewart was the first team to follow Ferrari's lead in moving the exhaust vents to the top of the engine cover. This was at the Belgian GP, with a design very similar to that of Maranello's cars with the exception of the visible exhaust pipe obliquely cut to direct the flow of hot air even higher.

# WILLIAMS

*FW21*

*FW20*

were down to the same component, the differential. When considering the season's poor results it should, however, be remembered that the Supertec engine used by Williams (together with Benetton and BAR) was less powerful than the units powering the leading teams. Based on the car that finished the '98 season and in practice retaining its wheelbase dimension, the FW21 also maintained other links such as the shape and height of the nose and the area in front of the rear wheels and the layout of the rear suspension. At the presentation of the car the height of the large barge-boards behind the front wheels never previously used by Williams caused comment. This feature lasted just one race. By Brazil the Williams were being raced without barge-boards and with the large vanes within the front suspension notably modified. It is interesting that this configuration came about by chance as during testing at Silverstone Ralf Schumacher lost a barge-board but noticed no difference in the FW21's handling. Wind tunnel testing led to the new aerodynamic package with no barge-boards that was adopted for the rest of the season. Williams was also the team responsible for introducing yet more ultra-expensive trickery in the form of slim bars of tungsten acting as ballast. This feature was actually used in the last 3 races of the '98 season but was only discovered and then imitated by all the leading teams at the start of the '99 championship. The tungsten was actually inserted within the wooden board, the lowest point on the car (see the "Underbodies" chapter, page 56), and as many teams had a margin of over 50 kg to play with it is easy to see why Patrick Head's innovation allowing the car's centre of gravity to be lowered was so eagerly seized upon.

The '99 season was Williams' worst in recent years. After conquering the World Championship title in '97 with Jacques Villeneuve they dropped back to third place in '98 and could manage no better than fifth in '99. This was the second consecutive season without a victory for the team led by Patrick Head yet the FW21, the second post-Newey car (after his move to McLaren in summer '97), had a number of interesting and unusual features, in contrast with the preceding car

that had appeared to be simply a development of the concepts initiated by Newey back in '97 with the FW17. The pairing of Gavin Fisher, design chief, and Geoff Willis, the aerodynamicist, produced a clean, compact car that raised eyebrows with two trend-bucking features: low side-pods and exhausts blowing in the lower part of the central tunnel. The first remained unchanged throughout the season, in spite of numerous modifications to the rear section of the pods them-

selves, while the second was the object of intensive development work that concluded at the British GP with the central vent abandoned in favour of the standard location at the end of the upper edge of the lateral channels. Equipped with a new longitudinal gearbox cast in light alloy, the FW21 proved to be unreliable, completing just 71% of the total laps over the season and finishing only 15 times from 32 starts. It suffered from 8 different technical problems, of which 4

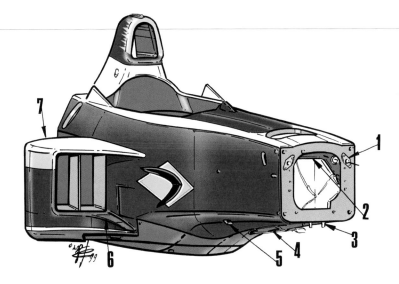

the Spanish GP (see "Underbodies" chapter, page 54) and definitively abandoned at the British GP in favour of the traditional position above the lateral channels (5). On this occasion the shape of the lateral channels (7, bottom drawing) was modified, the inverted-V (3, top drawing) being changed. Williams instead retained the lower wishbone (4) set in the air flow under the lateral channels all season, despite being the first team to free the channels in '95. At the San Marino GP raised external sections (6) to the lateral channels were introduced.

## CHASSIS

The FW21's chassis was extremely compact with very low side-pods, the front sections of which acted as deformable structures (7) while the radiator intake was raised with respects to the underbody (6). At the front can be seen the horizontal arrangement of the torsion bars that in '98 had been pivoted vertically inside the rocker. The central mount (2) of the lower wishbone (see drawing to side) could be detached to allow the suspension geometry to be modified easily. The lower part of the chassis was very rounded (4). Note (5) the rear mount of the lower wishbone.

## FRONT SUSPENSION

For the '99 season Williams too adopted the front suspension layout introduced in '98 by Ferrari and McLaren. The torsion bars (1) were now horizontal while the dampers (2) were vertical. Note the steering column (1) articulated so as not to interfere with the driver's feet. The lower wishbone mount was not integral with the chassis but attached with two small plates (4).

## REAR VIEW

This drawing compares the two exhaust layouts. At the top is the standard solution with the exhaust blowing very low (1) in the central tunnel, modified at

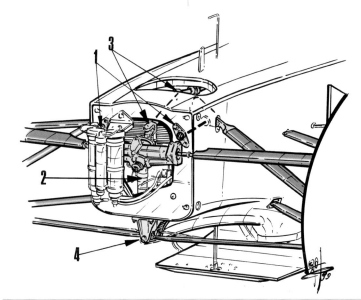

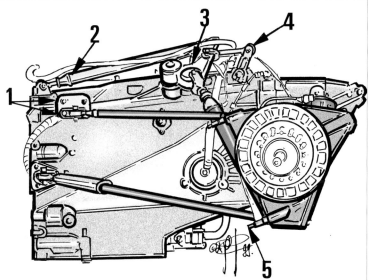

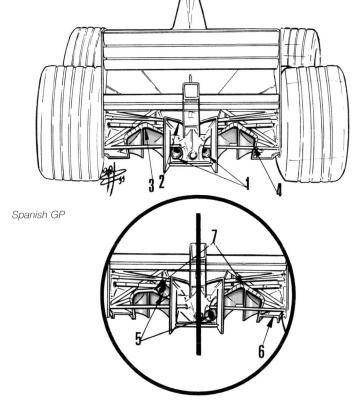

*Spanish GP*

## GEARBOX

The FW21 used a new very square and extremely compact gearbox cast in light alloys. Note the double wishbone mounts (1). The dampers were mounted in a horizontal V above the rear part, indicated in the drawing by the rods (2) used to lock the suspension during transit. Williams was one of the few teams still to retain traditional coil springs at the rear rather than torsion bars. At (3) can be seen the rocker to which the short anti-roll bar was attached (4). The brake calipers were attached to the lower part of the upright (5).

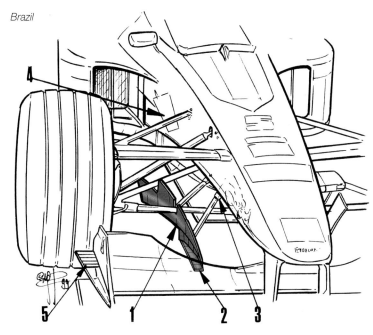

*Brazil*

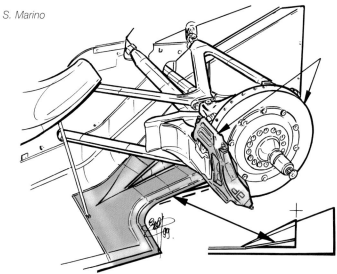

*S. Marino*

## BARGE-BOARDS

The large barge-boards behind the wheels were only used for the first race. They proved to have little influence on aerodynamic balance on the occasion of testing at Silverstone when Ralf Schumacher's car lost one without causing the driver any problems. The small vanes within the suspension were retained albeit in modified form.

## BRAZILIAN GP

In Brazil the FW21 raced without the large barge-boards (4) behind the wheels and with modified vanes within the suspension. These were longer (1) and had a horizontal knife-edge section (2) at the bottom (within the central 50 cm). The mounts (3) were also stiffened after the failures in Australia and during private testing at Silverstone. The small fins either side of the end-plates (5) were in a transparent material.

## SAN MARINO GP

At the San Marino GP Williams introduced an innovation to the "foot step" area within the rear wheels. This was no longer horizontal but inclined upwards as highlighted in the detail. This feature was subsequently copied by Ferrari for its ultra-fast track chutes (see "Underbodies" chapter, page 55). Williams also used the smaller, lighter version of the AP six-pot calipers along with smaller diameter discs.

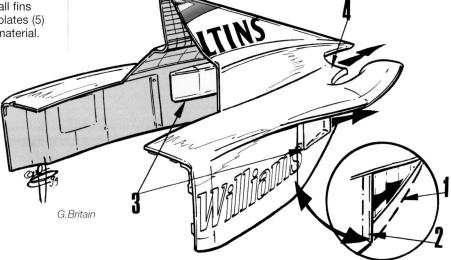

*G.Britain*

## BRITISH GP

The British GP represented an important stage in the development of the FW21. Exhausts blowing in the central tunnel were abandoned as shown on the preceding page, two bodywork variants were introduced with modifications at the rear. The vertical opening (2) with the bodywork recessed in the end section (1) was eliminated in favour of a version with diverse external vents (3). The end part (4) of the engine cover was widened to improve the extraction of hot air from the rear.

## AUSTRIAN GP

Experimentation with cast-iron brake discs (1) aroused great surprise as the material had not been used in F1 since way back in '85 apart from a brief test also conducted by Williams in '97. This led to in an increase in unsprung weight of no less than 9.2 kg when in theory this value should always be reduced to the minimum. The feature was introduced to satisfy Zanardi's demands and to allow the front tyres to warm up quickly. The suspension was also modified with lower arms equipped with a broader aerodynamic fairing (2).

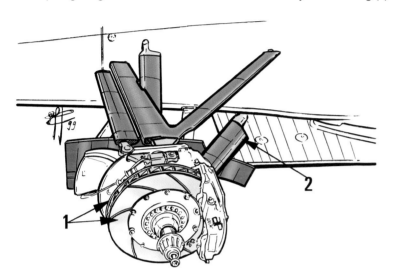

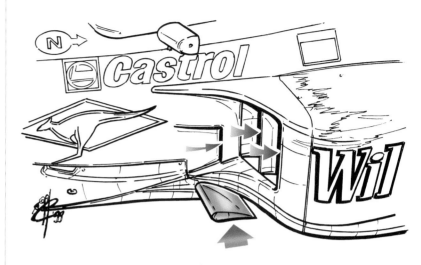

## BELGIAN GP

These fins in front of the side-pod intakes were inspired by those of the Jordans and adopted from the Belgian GP to optimise air flow in the central area of the car and to improve cooling.

## JAPANESE GP

At Suzuka a long vertical Gurney flap was fitted either side of the flat knife-edge section below the central section of the chassis to guarantee more downforce in this area lacking the large barge-boards in front of the side-pods used by almost all the teams except Jordan and Benetton. eccezione di Jordan e Benetton.

## HUNGARIAN GP

This new bodywork with enormous vents for hot air in the upper part was introduced at the Hungarian GP. It was not used in the race because while it ensured optimal heat loss it led to a notable increase in drag. It was instead used in the Malaysian GP.

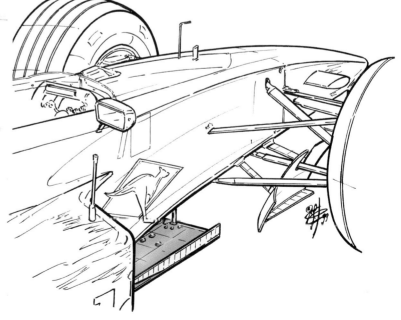

# BENETTON

This was another season to forget for Benetton as the team slipped a further place in the Constructors' Championship (from the 5th of '98 to 6th), recording just a single podium finish, Fisichella's 2nd place in Canada. The fault lay with a Nick Wirth design that was very ambitious on paper, but very uncompetitive on the track. Outwardly the B199 was very similar to the previous season's car, but was fitted with drive-shafts at the front due to the introduction of the revolutionary FTT braking system. In order to counter the 11 kg extra weight of this system

bearing on the front axle, the B199 emerged with the vast wheelbase dimension of 3,285 mm, around 200 mm longer than the average dimensions for the '99 season cars, Prost excepted (3,242 mm). In theory FTT, a form of differential controlling the torque acting on the front brakes, should have provided much better balanced and more efficient braking, but it almost immediately proved to be a useless weight handicap, especially for Wurz who of course weighs more than his team-mate Fisichella. The Austrian only used the system at the Brazilian GP and it was defin-

itively abandoned by the team from the 6th race of the season in Canada. The other technical secret, that of the twin clutch, also consumed precious development time for a car afflicted by notable aerodynamic tuning problems. The B199 was otherwise a banal reworking of the previous season's car in terms of its general layout and aerodynamics. It was in this sector that numerous experiments were performed with at least 7 front wing configurations with 7 different flaps, two types of main-plane and 6 different end-plate designs. At the rear there were 4 different wing variants: Montreal, Zeltweg, Hockenheim and Nürburgring. The small vanes within the front suspension reappeared at Hockenheim (the same as those used in '98 and then replaced with new elements). As for the suspension, at the rear the layout copied that of the B198 with classic coil-spring dampers and the possibility of mounting a third element used from the British GP onwards. There was a new front layout

inspired by the one introduced by Ferrari in '98 with two main vertical dampers and a third horizontal element located at the top between the two rockers. The B199 was equipped with hydraulic power steering from the first race of the season. Benetton was one of the 8 teams to adopt the new central oil reservoir location.

## COMPARISON '98 - '99

This form of montage highlights the macroscopic difference in wheelbase between the B199 (above) and the old B198 (below), almost 20 cm due to the weight of the FTT system bearing on the front axle. The comparison also reveals how the elongation was achieved by distancing the front axle from the body of the car, that is to say the side-pods.

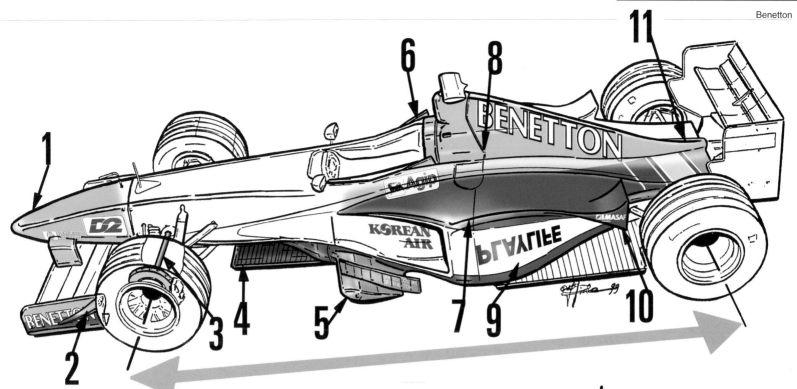

## B199

The B199 shared a certain family likeness with the B198 in terms of the shape of the nose and the side-pods, including the low protection structure either side of the cockpit. The most obvious difference concerned the increase in wheelbase (of around 20 cm) highlighted by the red arrow.

1) The nose was slightly longer and symmetrical with respects to that of the B198. 2) New end-plates of which no less than 6 variants were used during the season.

3) The front wheels have drive-

shafts connected to the brakes to control the braking force. The system accounted for an increase in weight of 11 kg. (9 due to the system itself and 2 to the strengthening of the chassis).

4) The increased wheelbase is also revealed by the lengthening of the knife-edge area below the chassis. 5) The controversial low protection structures at the sides of the chassis fitted to the B198 were retained. 6) Either side of the cockpit were fins to respect the dimensions of the structures protecting the driver's head. 7) The shorter

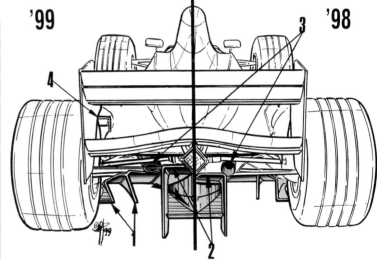

side-pods were notably higher and more rounded. 8) The oil tank was located between the chassis and the engine. 9) The narrowing of the rear section of the bodywork was more accentuated than on the B198. 10) The small fins in front of the rear wheels were very different. 11) The engine cover was slightly longer and lower.

## OIL RESERVOIR

Benetton adopted the central oil reservoir location with a very tall cylindrical tank. As seen in the drawing, the installation of the tank with the radiator packs facing backwards was very compact.

## REAR AND COMPARISON

The diffuser of the B199 was very similar to the one introduced in the second half of the season on the B198. The drawing instead compares the versions that opened the two seasons. On the right is the aerodynamics of the basic B198, on the left that of the B199. 1) The lateral channels had external and intermediate walls inclined inwards. 2) The central channel was higher and square. 3) The exhaust tail-pipes were flattened rather than round.
4) The fins on front of the wheel were different.

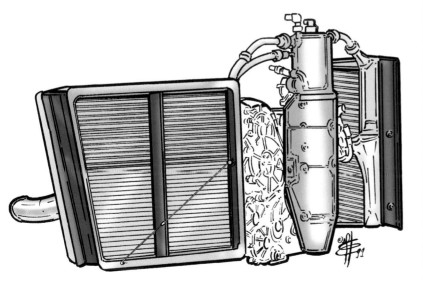

'98

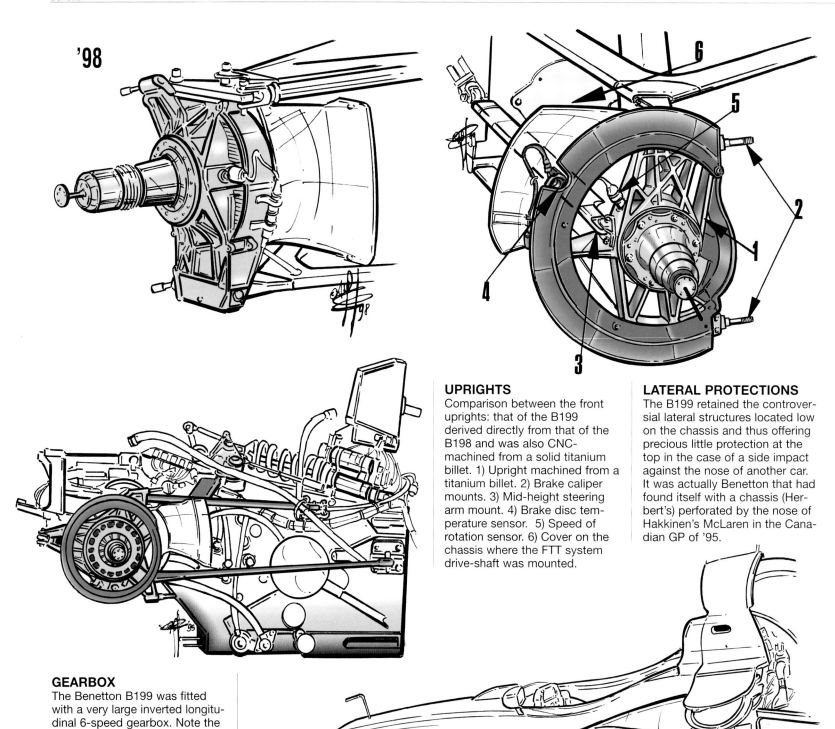

## UPRIGHTS
Comparison between the front uprights: that of the B199 derived directly from that of the B198 and was also CNC-machined from a solid titanium billet. 1) Upright machined from a titanium billet. 2) Brake caliper mounts. 3) Mid-height steering arm mount. 4) Brake disc temperature sensor. 5) Speed of rotation sensor. 6) Cover on the chassis where the FTT system drive-shaft was mounted.

## LATERAL PROTECTIONS
The B199 retained the controversial lateral structures located low on the chassis and thus offering precious little protection at the top in the case of a side impact against the nose of another car. It was actually Benetton that had found itself with a chassis (Herbert's) perforated by the nose of Hakkinen's McLaren in the Canadian GP of '95.

## GEARBOX
The Benetton B199 was fitted with a very large inverted longitudinal 6-speed gearbox. Note the spring and damper assembly mounted horizontally above the gearbox casting and the vicinity of the two suspension wishbones.

## FTT SYSTEM

Heavy and unreliable, the FTT system was in practice abandoned from the Canadian GP onwards. The drawing on the right highlights one of the half-shafts (1) linking the discs of the two front wheels to a kind of differential (cantilevered from the pedalbox). Also visible is the aerodynamically profiled steering arm (2). The drawing on the far right instead shows the front running gear without the FTT system. The dampers can be seen through the openings from which the half-shafts exited (1). The steering arm (2) is attached in the middle of the upright and the system is power assisted (3). 4) Cables to retain the wheels in the event of a crash. 5) Torsion bars removable from the front. 6) Anti-roll bar access port.

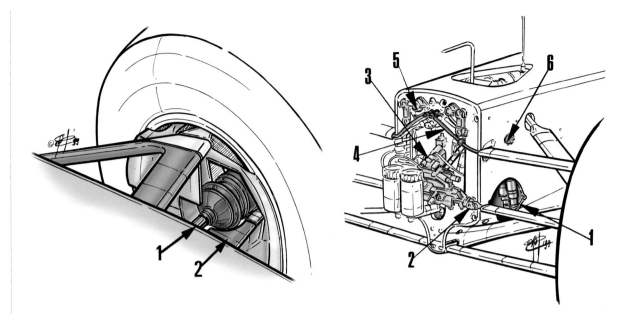

## FRONT SUSPENSION

The suspension of the B199 effectively mirrored the layout introduced by Ferrari in '98, with a small third horizontal damper (1) linked to the two rockers.

2) Anti-roll bar replacement port. 3) Plug to cover the passage for the drive-shafts (unused after the Canadian GP). 4) Brake disc thickness sensor. 5) Brake disc temperature sensor.

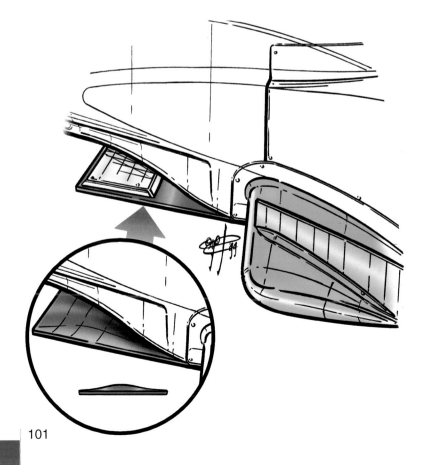

## KNIFE EDGE ZONE

Benetton frequently placed ballast in the knife-edge zone beneath the chassis. From the British GP the team introduced a new fairing with a slightly rounded shape in the centre, as highlighted in the circle at the bottom.

# PROST

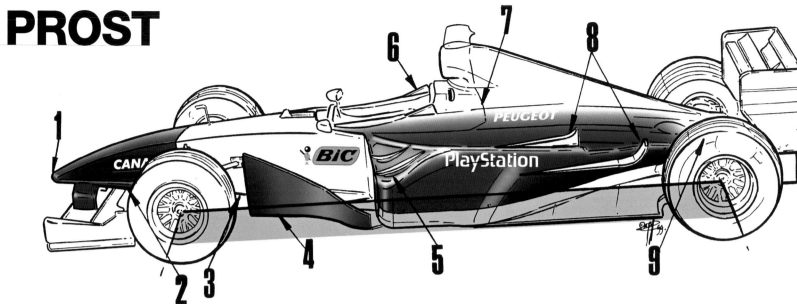

The second car constructed by Prost was as equally unconventional and individual as Louis Bigois's first effort. Unfortunately, however, it also retained the earlier car's lack of competitiveness strictly deriving from technical decisions made during the design phase. For a young team such as Prost it would have been wise to opt for a traditional but reliable car with high build standards following the disappointments of the previous season. The AP02 instead actually repeated the errors seen in the earlier AP01, being notably distant from the philosophies adopted by the other teams largely based on those of the successful McLaren. There were two negative aspects easily identifiable from the car's first appearances: the aerodynamic

package with complicated and rather inefficient features and the absurd wheelbase dimension of 324 cm, almost 20 cm greater than all the other cars with the exception of the Benetton (328 cm), but justified by the need to counterbalance the weight of the FTT system with a longer wheelbase and weight distribution biased towards the rear. The AP02 also proved to be a heavy car that was difficult to set up and unreliable. It suffered no less than 11 retirements from 32 starts due to mechanical problems, 5 of which were down to the Peugeot engine. Nonetheless the French team gained two places in the Constructors' Championship, finishing 7th thanks to Trulli's second place at the Nürburgring in the extraordinary GP of Europe won by Her-

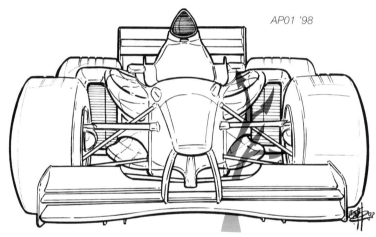

AP01 '98

bert in the Stewart. Below its massive but sophisticated bodywork the AP02 concealed features that were the fruit of the genius of John Barnard, engaged as a consultant. He was responsible for the new external master cylinder location in the lower part of the chassis and the creation of suspension with flexure mounts at the rear too (a feature introduced by Barnard on the front end of the Ferrari 412 T1 in '94 and then copied by many other teams).

### AP02

The side view of the second Prost immediately reveals its exaggerated wheelbase (underlined by the orange band) and the squared-off and rather inele-

gant shape of the side-pods scattered with fins of various sizes. 1) The high, pointed nose was abandoned in favour of a fairly low version V-shaped (2) at the bottom. 3) Knife-edge suspension mounts were used. 4) The large barge-boards were McLaren-inspired. 5) The side-pods were incredibly long and lost the rounded form of the AP01. They were characterised by the new fins mounted at the front. 6) Fins allowing the protection structure to be reduced in size were fitted either side of the cockpit. 7) The oil reservoir was located centrally as on the AP01. 8) New fins fitted to the rear of the side-pods too. 9) The clutch was no longer fitted to the back of the gearbox.

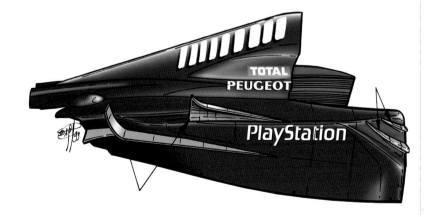

## AP01 '98

The first Prost was characterised by rounded lines with enormous side-pod air intakes in the form of NACA ducts. The nose was long and pointed.

## SIDE-PODS

The detail of the side-pods allows the new fins introduced by Prost to be highlighted. The first are at the entrance to the very square side-pods, the second dual fins replace the single upwardly curved element used by numerous other teams. The first fin is mounted in an advanced position beyond the area affected by the restriction of 50 cm in height from the reference place.

## REAR SUSPENSION

The rear suspension layout was very straightforward with the dampers (1) free of coil springs placed in V-formation over the gearbox. 2) The torsion bars pivoted on the rockers. 3) The anti-roll bars was located at the rear. 5) The twinned exhausts passed between the drive-shafts and the upper wishbones of the version used up to the Hungarian GP.

## HIGH EXHAUSTS

From the Belgian GP Prost adopted the high exhaust feature introduced by Ferrari in '98. Note the large heat shields placed either side of the cylinder head.

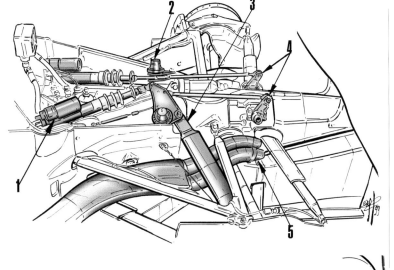

Again at the Italian GP, the bodywork was modified with an extension of the rear section as far as the rear wing support and a supplementary hot air vent in the lower area beneath the long fin. This last feature had already been used for those races held in very hot conditions.

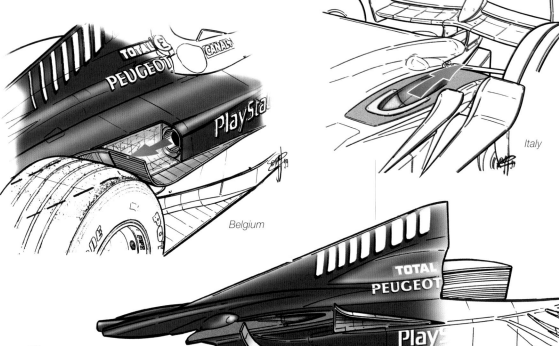

*Belgium*

*Italy*

## BELGIAN GP - ITALIAN GP

The first version of the high exhausts comprised an unusual lateral vent in front of the rear wheels, very different to the layouts adopted by Ferrari. This feature was abandoned from the successive Italian GP where the Prost had exhaust vents identical to those of the Ferrari and the Stewart. that had joined the small group at the Belgian GP.

# SAUBER

*C18*

*C17 '98*

In its third consecutive season with the Ferrari V10, Sauber had been expected to provide confirmation of its technical potential but instead the 1999 championship was a veritable disaster for the Swiss team. From the sixth place achieved in '98, it plunged to eighth in the final table, without ever recording a podium finish (Alesi finished 3rd in Belgium in '98) and collecting just five sixth-place finishes. The fault lay with a car, the C 18, that proved to be the least reliable of the entire field, completing just 60% of the race laps making up the F1 season, with just 11 finishes from 32 starts. The principal cause of the retirements was the new inverted longitudinal gearbox, equipped with a clutch at the rear rather than in the traditional location between engine and gearbox. This feature, which had also been responsible for many of Prost's problems in '98, left the Sauber drivers stranded no less than 7 times. Diniz also set the unwelcome record for the number of crashes

and spins: no less than 29 against his team-mate Alesi's 20. The car produced by the staff directed by Leo Rees immediately gave an impression of being a simple development of the previous season's car of which it retained the basis of the aerodynamic package. The C17's unique side-pods with asymmetric intakes disappeared, while the suspension was also different, the McLaren '98 layout being adopted with horizontal torsion bars at the front and, above all, low-set steering arms. The small protuberances on the top of the nose that on the C17 contained the vertical torsion bars were thus also eliminated. The Sauber was the only car to use extensions linking the flaps in front of the rear wheels to the rear wing end-plates at all of the circuits.

## C18

The C18 retained the high nose and the general layout of the '98 car. 1) The front wing retained planes with the central section raised higher from the ground. The new rearwards sloping wing support allowed a very long nose to be employed. 2) The front wing end-plates with convex external sections equipped with a small fin were new. 3) Sauber was the team which used the lowest steering arm location. 4) The pushrod mount was faired. 5) In the area

in front of the cockpit there was a small step that directed turbulence away from the driver's helmet. 6) Early in the season the barge-boards behind the front wheels were very large extending in a sinuous form towards the area within the front suspension. 7) The side-pod intakes were symmetrical and set close to the survival cell. 8) The engine air intake was triangular. 9) Sauber was able to count on Ferrari engines for the third consecutive season. 10) Small flaps were retained in front of the rear wheels throughout the season. 11) Sauber was the only team to use the bodywork extensions linking the end-plates of the rear wing on the ultra-fast tracks too.

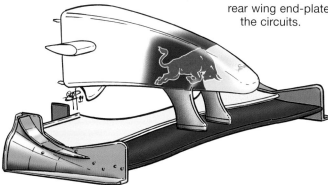

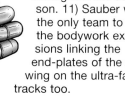

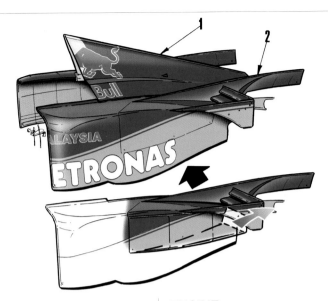

## SAUBER '98

The asymmetric side-pod intakes that characterised the C17, highlighted by red arrow, were abandoned on the C18. The small protuberances (blue) concealing the vertical torsion bars also disappeared, the bars being horizontal on the C18.

## ENGINE

In '99 Sauber was provided with the engine that had proved to be one of the most powerful and reliable units in '98, the 10-cylinder Ferrari O48. The installation did not, however, feature the high exhausts introduced by Ferrari at the Spanish GP.

modified easily. Alongside the drawing can be seen the version with larger hot air vents introduced in Brazil and used at all the hottest circuits.

## BARGE-BOARDS

During the season three different barge-board designs were used. The first extended forwards within the front suspension and was divided into two elements. The second, introduced at Monaco, was shorter but of the same height. The third, introduced at Zeltweg, was lower. They all curved inwards at the bottom obliging the adoption of a small downwards projection (highlighted in yellow).

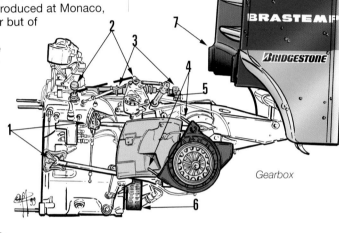

*Gearbox*

## GEARBOX

The gearbox was Sauber's weakness in '99, in part due to the location of the clutch (6) at the back rather than the front between the engine and gearbox. 1) The suspension wishbones had vertical mounts to reduce friction. 2) The dampers were mounted horizontally (indicated by the dotted line). 3) There was a central third bump-stop element. 4) The brake calipers were mounted on the upper front part

of the upright. 5) The anti-roll bar was linked to the rocker by two small rods. 7) The rear wing endplates, twisted at the front, were linked to the long extensions visible in the drawing below.

## ROLL BAR

In the dramatic incident at the start of the GP of Europe, Diniz's Sauber overturned at the relatively modest speed of around 90 kph and literally lost the roll bar. This failure encouraged the FIA to increase the loading on the roll bar in the crash tests for the 2000 season. The Brazilian driver emerged unscathed from the crash, thanks to the height of the survival cell in the area to the sides of the cockpit (indicated by the red arrow).

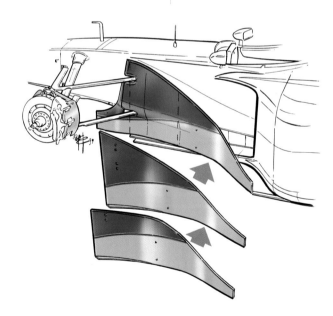

## NOSE

The sharply inclined front wing support allowed the nose to be lengthened. Note the sinuous shape of the planes, the main-plane in blue, the full-width flap in yellow. On the ultra-fast tracks Sauber adopted twinned flaps (see the Noses chapter, page 53).

## SIDE-PODS

Sauber always used the long extensions linking the flaps in front of the rear wheels with the rear wing end-plates visible in the drawing (2). The decision to produce the bodywork in three sections (1) allowed the shape of the rear part of the side-pods to be

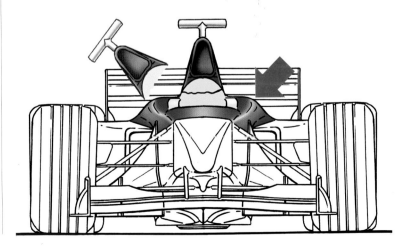

# ARROWS

*A20*

*A19 '98*

Arrows was the only team to participate in the 1999 F1 World Championship with the car it had used the previous season, the A20, designed by John Barnard before he moved to Prost in July, '98. The team was therefore unable to maintain its excellent seventh place in the Constructors' Championship, but did manage to beat the new-born Bar and, like Minardi, to conquer a championship point, this despite a «home-made» engine (derived from the Hart V10) that was undoubtedly the least powerful in the field. Responsibility for development of the design passed to Mike Coughlan, the British magician's former right-hand man, who immediately put into effect one of the modifications planned the previous year, the lengthening of the wheelbase. This was achieved in the simplest and least expensive manner possible, by giving a different inclination to the suspension arms so as to gain an extra 75 mm that extended the wheelbase from 2,950 mm to 3,025 mm, compa-

rable with the extensions made by the team's rivals in '98. Despite being based on a year-old design, the A20 was extremely interesting, having retained the multiple innovations introduced by Barnard as well as the appeal of the clean, attractive lines of the basic car. At first sight, the most conspicuous modification concerned the fins in front of the rear wheels linked to the large radiator air vents (as seen in the colour drawing compared with the '98 car). The new features introduced the previous season concerned above all the aerodynamic package, with unique side-pods characterised by a very high forward section and vents for the hot air in the upper part in front of the rear wheels. This feature attracted immediate criticism but actually inspired the high exhausts introduced by Ferrari and, above all, a similar feature adopted on the new McLaren MP4/14. The suspension configurations were new in '98, with the front layout remaining in '99 too the only example of vertical torsion bars and with horizontal dampers visible in the upper part of the chassis. The previous season Ferrari and McLaren had introduced a new layout with horizontal bars and vertical dampers, copied in '99 by almost all the other teams. As for the rear suspension, it is sufficient to recall that it was also a source of inspiration for the all-conquering McLaren with regards the vertical relocation of the torsion bars outside the

gearbox. One of the innovations for the '99 season, the carbonfibre gearbox casing, instead failed to convince. Barnard and Jenkins (Stewart '98) had contested the primacy of having introduced the feature first, but while the Scottish team abandoned the concept in view of the '99 season, Arrows opted to persevere, paying the price in terms of mechanical reliability. No less than 8 out of 17 retirements were down to the gearbox.

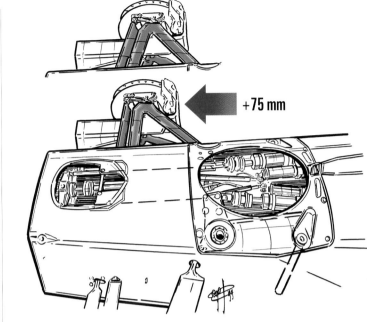

## FRONT SUSPENSION

The front suspension layout remained unchanged with the exposed horizontal dampers located in a large niche in the upper part of the chassis. The torsion bars were vertical but placed further forwards, beyond the area off-limits to suspension elements specified by the FIA. The only innovation concerned the different (forwards) inclination of the suspension arms to permit a lengthening of the wheelbase by 75 mm.

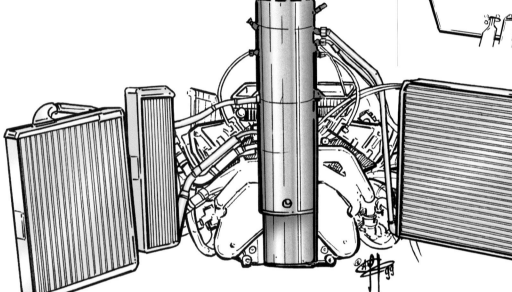

## OIL RESERVOIR

One of the most interesting innovations introduced for the '98 season by Barnard at the same time as Jenkins on the Stewart, was the central location of the oil reservoir. This feature was then taken up by no less than 8 teams in the '99 season and is destined to become universally adopted in the first championship of the new millennium. The configuration adopted by Arrows featured a very tall titanium cylinder. The new location allowed piping to the radiating elements located close to the centre of gravity to be reduced to a minimum.

## REAR SUSPENSION

The rear end of the Arrows remained identical to that of the '98 car, from the elegant and compact carbonfibre gearbox to the suspension layout. The location of the torsion bar outside the gearbox is highlighted by the arrow. It is set further forwards with respects to the suspension rocker to which it is connected by a link as at the front. Adrian Newey used a similar external location for the torsion bar (but coaxial with the rocker) in the rear suspension layout of the MP4/14 that carried Hakkinen to his second World Championship title.

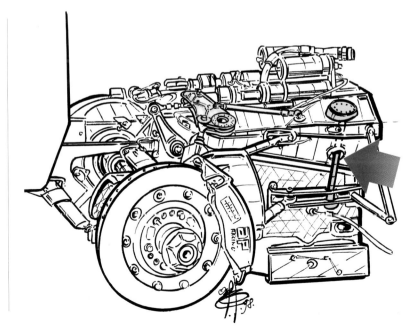

# MINARDI

The first car designed under the direction of Gustav Brunner, recruited from Ferrari in the summer of '98 and assisted by Gabrielle Tredozi, proved to be technically very interesting but slightly under-developed and thus spent the season trying to catch up. The single Constructors' Championship point conquered allowed the team from Faenza to finish the season on an equal footing with Arrows and ahead of the big-budget but new-born BAR. The objectives were those of building a very light car with extremely high stiffness values for each component. Weight distribution with around 45% bearing on the front axle was obtained thanks to the placing of heavy ballast towards the front. A figure of 50 kg has been mentioned, a notable achievement for what is indisputably a minor team equipped, moreover, with one of the least powerful and heaviest engines on the grid, the 10-cylinder Ford used by Stewart in '98. The driver was set as far back as possible, as were the side-pods, although these were slightly longer than on the '98 car obliged to have low set external protection structures (highlighted in the drawing below). The very compact M01 was the car with the shortest wheelbase in the '99 championship, the only one that came under the 3-metre threshold at 2,950 mm. This dimension was actually modified as early as the third race, the San Marino GP, with the front axle being moved forward by 60 mm, firstly on Badoer's car, and then from the

next race on all three cars. Minardi too had a secret to conceal in the '99 season: rear suspension equipped with a very unusual movement (documented in the "Suspension" chapter), in contrast with the front layout which appeared to be a simple development of the one adopted by McLaren and Ferrari in '98. At the rear the torsion bars were very long and located horizontally outside the gearbox while the vertical dampers were instead concealed inside. The least advanced aspect of the design was the very simple aerodynamic package which fell into line with the trends that emerged during the '98 sea-

son. Frequently side-lined by gearbox problems (causing 5 retirements) at the start of the season, Minardi eventually completed the 7th highest

number of race laps but unfortunately was also the team, together with Arrows, that completed the least number of private testing days (31) during the year.

## MINARDI M01

The M01 retained the high nose of the '98 car while the lines were clean and square-cut. Large barge-boards appeared behind the front wheels, while the controversial low protection structures outside the side-pods, visible in the circle at the bottom, were eliminated. The front suspension featured steering arms located in the middle of the uprights, as on the '98 McLaren. The narrowing of the lower bodywork equipped with simple fins in front of the rear wheels was highly accentuated. The bodywork could be divided into three parts with a sharply tapering, narrow engine cover and was modified and lengthened for the Austrian GP.

## SURVIVAL CELL

The M01's survival cell was very simple and straightforward with the front section almost free of access holes to the pedal box in the interest of maximum rigidity. Note the slight widening of the fuel tank area. The deformable cockpit protection structures occupied the whole of the front part of the side-pods.

## SURVIVAL CELL REAR

Minardi adopted the central oil reservoir location at the rear of the survival cell as highlighted in the drawing. The shape of this area practically replicates that of the oil reservoir itself. The drawing shows the two hatches for refuelling and the engine mounts (yellow).

## OIL RESERVOIR

In practice, together with the Ford engine the Minardi inherited the central oil reservoir location introduced by Stewart in '98. The team created a completely new shape, however, no longer tall and narrow, but rather squat and hexagonal so as to sit perfectly in the housing created at the rear of the survival cell.

## BRAKE BLEEDING

While starting out with a very simple basic design, Minardi presented a number of minor refinements such as the brake bleeding system. The mechanics no longer had to remove the nose as on all the other cars because access to the small fluid reservoir was guaranteed by two small apertures at the top of the chassis, as shown in the drawing.

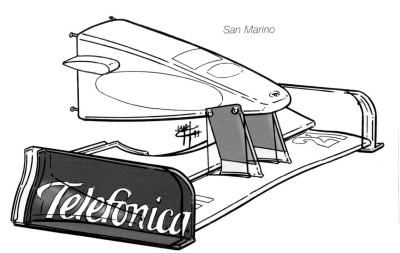

*San Marino*

## SAN MARINO GP

From the San Marino GP the wheelbase was extended by 60 mm thanks to the forward inclination of the front suspension arms. To avoid building a new nose that would have to be crash tested, the central supports of the front wing were modified, inclined in such a way as to maintain the same distance from the front wheels set by the regulations. The extension is highlighted in yellow in this drawing.

# BAR

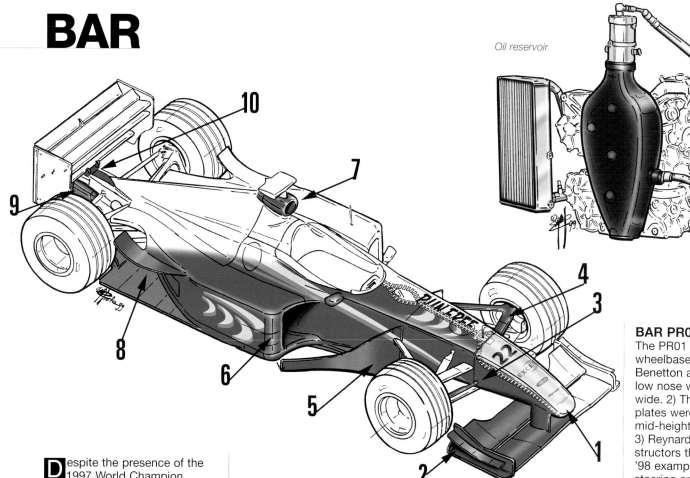

*Oil reservoir*

Despite the presence of the 1997 World Champion, Jacques Villeneuve, BAR's debut season in Formula 1 was extremely disappointing. Even taking into account the allowances which inevitably have to be made for a new team, the car designed by the staff at Reynard made a mockery of even the most pessimistic predictions. Reasonably competitive over a single lap, from the very first race it proved to be unreliable and rather fragile. Out of 32 starts, in fact, a BAR finished a race on only 8 occasions, collecting 18 retirements for technical motives (5 of which down to the clutch), 6 accidents with two chassis written off, the first at the second race in Brazil (Zonta missed three races with fractured legs) and a total of 30 spins and off-track excursions shared between the two drivers. Only in one area was BAR up with the leaders and that was in the number of chassis constructed over the course of the season: 8 like Ferrari and McLaren. Jacques Villeneuve joined the select band of World

Champions to have failed to conquer a single point in a championship season: Phil Hill in '63 with ATS, Graham Hill in '73 with Shadow and James Hunt in '79 with Wolf. Still on the negative side, BAR bettered only Sauber as the team that completed the second lowest number of race laps: 62% of the possible 2,000 laps comprising the 16 GPs making up the season. The fault lay with a car built by staff led by Malcom Oastler who were feeling their way in F1 and had opted for performance rather than a solid base for subsequent development. With its rather long wheelbase and side-pods and the driver seated further forwards than in the leading cars, the PR01 revealed a notable constructional fragility but no significant technical innovations. The series of negative performances began with the opening race in Australia when the rear wing support

failed and culminated in a dramatic weekend at Spa with two frightening qualifying crashes involving both drivers. While the drivers emerged unhurt, the situation was more serious for the team as one chassis had been destroyed and another damaged. This meant that one of the cars destined for later private testing at Monza (see chassis table) had to be assembled as a race car. Numerous modifications were made during the season and can be divided into two groups: those aimed at improving reliability (suspension, cooling, clutch and rear wing supports) and those in the field of aerodynamics, with important changes introduced at Imola with a diffuser profile and at Budapest with new side-pods.

## BAR PR01

The PR01 had the third longest wheelbase in the field, following Benetton and Prost. 1) The fairly low nose was flat and rather wide. 2) The front wing end-plates were new with a small, mid-height, squared-off flap. 3) Reynard was one of the constructors that followed McLaren's '98 example and mounted the steering arms in the middle of the uprights. 4) The upper wishbones were made of aerodynamically-sectioned carbonfibre. 5) The BAR was presented with large barge-boards behind the front wheels but a much lower version was adopted during the season. 6) The side-pods were very long and square-cut. 7) The engine air intake was oval in shape, similar to that of the Williams FW13B of 1990. 8) Two long, slim flip-ups were mounted in front of the rear wheels. 9) The diffuser profile comprised a very long central section and two lateral channels each with two vertical walls. 10) Particular attention was paid to the reinforcement of the rear wing support which failed on a number of occasions.

## OIL RESERVOIR

The carbonfibre oil reservoir, located centrally as it was on 7 cars in '99, was fairly tall and had an unusual amphora-like shape. The radiator packs were set in fan formation pointing backwards.

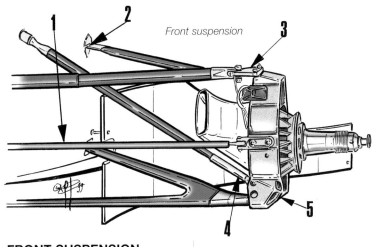

*Front suspension*

*Hungary*

## FRONT SUSPENSION

BAR introduced a new feature to F1 with the strut (4) attached directly to the upright (5) rather than the lower wishbone (see Suspension chapter). The team instead adopted the low steering link mounting (1) introduced on the MP4/13. Knife-edge wishbone mounts (2) were used whereas the mounts on the upright utilised a small plate (3).

## SAN MARINO GP

A modified diffuser profile made its debut on the PR01 at Imola.
1) In practice the upper end section of the central tunnel (highlighted in yellow) was cut away.
2) A small knife-edge zone remained in the lower part of the channel which had slightly divergent lateral walls. 3) BAR was the only team to use two vertical walls in the lateral channels. 4) The flaps added to the lower plane were doubled.

## BARGE-BOARDS

BAR began the season with large barge-boards behind the front wheels, tapering to a point at the top and featuring a hole for the passage of the front suspension arms due to their considerable length. A second version was introduced at Monaco that was lower and slightly shorter. The two were used alternately according to the track characteristics.

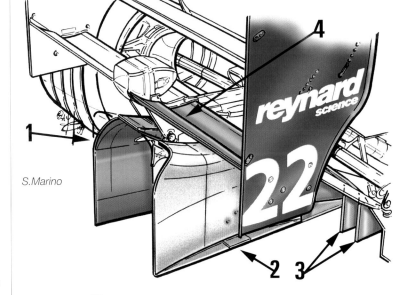

*S.Marino*

## HUNGARIAN GP

New bodywork was introduced at Budapest. The BAR's engine cover was divided into three sections. The central element was unchanged while the sides were completely redesigned. In the drawing the new version is mounted while the old squarer cover is depicted separately.
1) It is immediately apparent that the shape is much rounder and taller in the peripheral area, as on the F399. 2) New flip-ups in front of the rear wheels were equipped with two small vertical fins.
3) The lower part was also new with different hot air vent designs.

## GEARBOX

One of the PR10's weaknesses was the gearbox-rear wing support assembly. The first was a light alloy casting while the second was made in carbonfibre and passed the obligatory crash test when the cars were already in Australia for the first race of the season. 2) Fabricated upright with the upper wishbone mount on the carbonfibre structure.
3) The rear suspension wishbones were in steel.

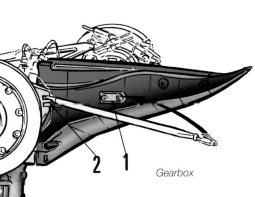

*Gearbox*

**Giorgio Nada Editore S.r.l.**

| | |
|---|---|
| Editorial coordination | Antonio Maffeis<br>Sergio Nada |
| Product development | Studio Enigma |
| Graphic design and cover | Agostino Carabelli |
| Translation | Neil Davenport |
| Contributors | Enrico Benzing (engines - tyres)<br>Paolo Rondelli (computer graphic)<br>Aimone Bolliger (DTP) |

Printed in Italy
by Grafiche d'Auria - Ascoli Piceno
June, 2000

© 2000 Giorgio Nada Editore,
Vimodrone (Milano)

Giorgio Nada Editore
Via Claudio Treves,15/17
I - 20090 VIMODRONE MI
Tel. +39 02 27301126
Fax +39 02 27301454
E-mail: nadamail@work-net.it
http://www.giorgionadaeditore.it

The catalogue of Giorgio Nada Editore publications is available on request at the address above.

Formula 1 '99 - Technical Analysis

ISBN: 88-7911-216-3